# 1 KINGS & 1 CHRONICLES

## A SELF-STUDY GUIDE

D0869126

## Irving L. Jensen

**MOODY PRESS**

CHICAGO

# Contents

# Introduction

The four books of Kings and Chronicles track Israel's history generally from the time of the division of the nation after the death of King Solomon into (1) the two tribes under Rehoboam and his successors, known as Judah, and (2) the ten tribes under Jeroboam and his successors, known as Israel. They reveal the failure of man and the failure of human governments, and point forward to that age when God will set up His own kingdom, with the greater Son of David as its sovereign head and all nations subject to Him.

Keep in mind that all that happened to God's people in those days should serve as examples to us and are written for our admonition (1 Cor. 10:11). God says that all Scripture is profitable for doctrine, for reproof, for correction, and for instruction in righteousness (2 Tim. 3:16). As we study these books, may each one learn the lessons that the Holy Spirit would teach him, that we may profit thereby. These lessons may be used either for individual Bible study or for classwork. I have included many charts in this new study edition to help the reader organize the lesson materials. The historical and survey charts enable one to visualize the place of each of the many facts in the large movements of Bible history, and the analytical charts help in recording paragraph-by-paragraph observations of the Bible text.

*When several are studying together*
*it would be well for the leader to observe the following:*

1. If any lesson seems too long for one meeting, assign half the lesson's work and leave the other half for the next meeting. Undertake no more than the class can do thoroughly.

2. Enlarged copies of the map and of some of the charts would be of help to the leader in the class sessions.

3. Insist that members of the class study the lesson at home and bring to the class written answers to the printed questions, insofar as possible.

4. Urge class members to read the assigned chapters in the Bible before they read the comments on them.

5. At the beginning of each meeting briefly review the previous work.

6. Insist that the members of the class think and study for themselves. Give them opportunities to express their thoughts and tell the lessons they have learned. Refuse to simply lecture to the class.

7. Constantly emphasize the importance of looking up all Scripture references given in each lesson. This should not be neglected.

8. Discuss among yourselves the following suggestions for Bible study, as given by Dwight L. Moody:

(a) Read the Bible as intelligently as you would read anything else.

(b) Do not read too fast or too much.

(c) Have some definite object in view.

(d) Learn to feed yourself.

# Lesson 1
# Background and General Introduction

This study guide concerns the book of 1 Kings and its parallel passages in Chronicles. The next study guide treats 2 Kings and 2 Chronicles. Because most of the background and general introductory material is common to all four books of Kings and Chronicles, that material is presented in the opening lesson of this manual.

It is important to become thoroughly acquainted with the background and general contents of the four books of Kings and Chronicles before analyzing any of their individual parts. Spend much time in your study of this lesson. It would be best to study the lesson in more than the one unit in order to give more attention to the subjects presented.

## I. BACKGROUND

### A. The Four Periods of Israel's History

As shown in the study manual of 1 and 2 Samuel, the history of Israel as given in the Old Testament falls into four periods, which may be remembered by four words, each beginning with the letter "C": Camp, Commonwealth, Crown, and Captivity. Study the accompanying chart.

1. *The Camp Period* extended from the call of Abraham, the founder of the nation of Israel, to Moses' bringing up the people to the "gate" of Canaan, a period of about 660 years. This history is given in the Pentateuch.

2. *The Commonwealth Period* extended from Israel's entrance into Canaan under Joshua to the crowning of their first king, Saul, a period of about 360 years. This history is given in Joshua, Judges, and Ruth.

6

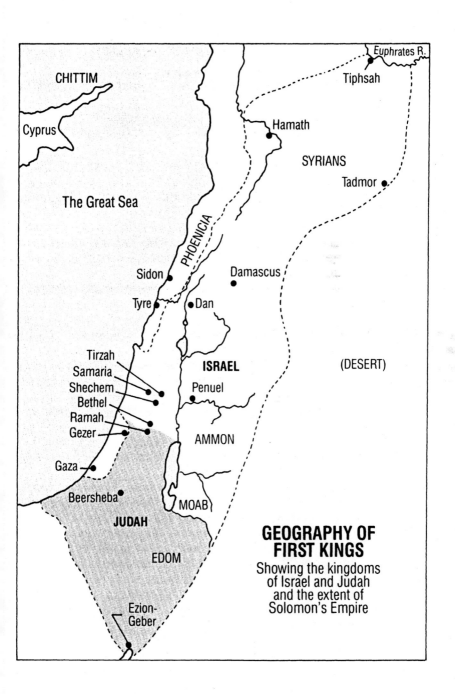

**GEOGRAPHY OF FIRST KINGS**

Showing the kingdoms of Israel and Judah and the extent of Solomon's Empire

| 1 | 2 | 3 | 4 |
|---|---|---|---|
| CAMP | COMMONWEALTH | CROWN | CAPTIVITY |
| 660 YEARS | 360 YEARS | 460 YEARS | 160 YEARS |
| PENTATEUCH | JOSHUA<br>JUDGES<br>RUTH | 1 & 2 ⎰ SAMUEL<br>KINGS<br>⎱ CHRONICLES | EZRA<br>NEHEMIAH<br>ESTHER |

3. *The Crown Period* extended from the crowning of their first king, Saul, to the Babylonian captivity, a period of about 460 years. This history is given in the six books of Samuel, Kings, and Chronicles.

4. *The Captivity Period* included the restoration and extended from the Babylonian Captivity to the end of the Old Testament history, a period of about 160 years. Ezra, Nehemiah, and Esther record this history.

Now let us look more closely at the Crown Period, which is the era covered by Kings and Chronicles.

## B. The Crown Period

Turn to the chart of Kings and Prophets on pages 102-3, observing that the Crown Period began in 1043 B.C., with the crowning of King Saul, and ended in 586 B.C., with the Babylonian Captivity.

Familiarize yourself with this chart by reading the explanation given thereon, and bear in mind, as you study the books of Kings and Chronicles, the three distinct divisions of the Crown Period, that is, the united kingdom, the divided kingdom, and the surviving kingdom (Judah).

Observe the prominence of the prophets during the kingdom years. The prophets of the first half of the Divided Kingdom period, among whom were Elijah and Elisha, did not write any prophetical books of the Old Testament. They were succeeded in the prophetic office by such great prophets as Isaiah and Jeremiah, known by the books they wrote. Kings and Chronicles furnish a background for the prophetic utterances, and, vice versa, the prophetic books shed much light on Kings and Chronicles. All the prophets were spokesmen for God, proclaiming His will to the covenant nation.

## C. The Books

1. *Titles and place in the canon.* The title "Kings" is appropriate, since the books record events in the careers of the kings of Judah and Israel, from Solomon to the last of the kings (Zedekiah). The title "Chronicles" originated with Jerome, who believed this represented the contents of the books better than the Hebrew title, meaning "The Accounts of the Days." As will be shown later, Chronicles has a deeper purpose than merely recording the historical events ("chronicles") of the period. From this standpoint the title may be misleading.

The locations of the books in the canon of Scripture are shown in the following table:

| EARLY HEBREW BIBLE | GREEK SEPTUAGINT | ENGLISH BIBLE | |
|---|---|---|---|
| | 3 KINGDOMS[1] | 1 KINGS | |
| | 4 KINGDOMS | 2 KINGS | " |
| | 1 CHRONICLES | 1 CHRONICLES | " |
| | 2 CHRONICLES | 2 CHRONICLES | " |

One reason for the Greek translation's breaking up of the Hebrew Bible's two books Kings and Chronicles into four books was because of the larger scroll space demanded by the translated versions. These splits have been carried over into the English versions of the Bible.

2. *Dates written, and authors.* In view of the unity of Kings, there apparently was only one author for 1 and 2 Kings. Since the latest item of 2 Kings (release of Jehoiachin) took place around 562 B.C., and since no mention is made of the return from Babylon (536 B.C.), 1 and 2 Kings were probably written between 562 and 536 B.C. Tradition has assigned Jeremiah as the author. Most authorities prefer the viewpoint of anonymity and agree that the writer was a Jewish captive in Babylon.

Various evidences point to the fact that Chronicles and Ezra were originally one consecutive history (e.g., compare 2 Chron. 36:22-23 and Ezra 1:1-3*a*). The books were written around 450 B.C., and it is likely that the author was Ezra.

1. 1 and 2 Samuel were called 1 and 2 Kingdoms in the Septuagint.

## II. GENERAL INTRODUCTION

### A. Contents of Kings and Chronicles

"The story that 1 Kings tells is that of a nation passing from affluence and influence to poverty and paralysis," according to G. Campbell Morgan.[2] We see here a nation, having rejected Jehovah from being King, attempting to govern itself and failing utterly.

Most of the chapters of Kings and Chronicles relate events of the Crown Period of Israel and Judah. This is shown by the following diagram:

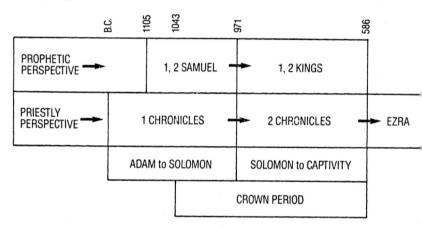

Observe that 1 Kings continues the narrative where 2 Samuel stops, and Ezra continues the narrative where 2 Chronicles stops. Although Kings and Chronicles generally cover the same period, the narratives are written from different perspectives. The differences will be discussed later.

There are great lines of truth common to both Kings and Chronicles. Three of these will be mentioned here: 1. *The two forms of government.* H. J. Carpenter has said, "The divine intention for the nation of Israel was that it should not be a monarchy but a theocracy. The KING of Judah and Israel was Jehovah—unrecognized very often—despised, ignored, rebelled against, but nevertheless, the ever-abiding KING."

When God chose Israel to be His representative people, delivered them from Egypt and brought them into the land of Canaan, His plan was that He should be not only their GOD, the One

---

2. G. Campbell Morgan, *Living Messages of the Books of the Bible* (Westwood, N.J., Revell, 1912), p. 177.

whom they would worship and recognize as their Saviour from death and bondage, but also their KING, the One whom they would implicitly obey. For a time He was given this place by the nation. His authority was unquestioned, and His miracles were gratefully recognized.

During the period covered by the books of Joshua and Judges, however, the people frequently failed to trust and obey their divine King. But whenever the nation transgressed His law, and thereby brought down divine chastisement in the form of invasion or oppression by their enemies, their King miraculously empowered a man to deliver Israel. These men were called judges, and through these men Jehovah continued His personal government of Israel. The climax of disobedience came before the death of Samuel, the last of the judges, when the nation of Israel rebelled against the kingship of God. Read 1 Samuel 8:4-7, and note especially God's words to Samuel: "They have not rejected thee, but they have rejected me, that I should not reign over them."

At that time God gave the people their desire and allowed them to have human kings, but it was not His first plan for them. As a result, for the next few hundred years the nation reaped turmoil, desolation, and threat of captivity. During this time God spoke to His people through the prophets, offering again to be their King, and reminding them that their troubles stemmed from their request for human kings. (Read Hos. 13:9-11.)

2. *The two thrones.* In the study of the books before us, the thrones on *earth* will be much in view. We shall be told what the various kings who occupied these earthly thrones said, did, and thought. However, the throne in *heaven* is also discerned, and from these books we shall learn much of what the one King who occupies the heavenly throne said, did, and thought. "Thus saith the Lord, The heaven is my throne, and the earth is my footstool" (Isa. 66:1). "The Lord's throne is in heaven: his eyes behold, his eyelids try, the children of men" (Ps. 11:4).

3. *The two kinds of prophets.* There were in Israel, during the period covered by the books of Kings and Chronicles, two distinct classes of prophets (just as there are today two distinct classes of preachers). There were the true prophets of God: men whom God had called to the office, to whom He gave a message to proclaim to the people, and who faithfully performed the work that God had set them to do, regardless of public opinion, persecution, or ridicule.

Then there were false prophets: men who called themselves prophets of God, who professed to have a message from God but who spoke only what the people wanted to hear rather than what they needed to hear. They were men who refused to preach against sin and exhort the people to turn to God in repentance as their only hope of salvation from ruin. They were those who cried, "Peace, peace," when there was no peace.

For the names of the true prophets who faithfully delivered God's messages during this period of Israel's history, turn to the Chart of Kings and Prophets on pages 102-3. This chart indicates also when these prophets lived and did their work, and who were the kings reigning at the time of their ministry. It will greatly help you to keep this chart before you as you study Kings and Chronicles.

### B. Contrasts of Kings and Chronicles

The relationship of Chronicles to Kings is similar to the relationship of the gospel of John to the Synoptic Gospels: While identical events are recorded in both, the later books do more in the way of interpretation and reflection. For example, Kings narrates the political and royal fortunes of the nation, whereas Chronicles looks at these in the light of the sacred and ecclesiastical. The following tabulation shows other contrasts:

| KINGS | CHRONICLES |
|---|---|
| 1. prophetic perspective (e.g., judgments) | priestly perspective (e.g., hopes) |
| 2. wars very prominent | Temple very prominent |
| 3. the fortunes of the thrones | continuity of the Davidic line |
| 4. record of both Israel and Judah | record primarily of Judah |
| 5. morality | redemption |

### C. Purposes of Kings and Chronicles

In view of their contents, it may be said that the main purpose of these books is not simply to record the facts of Hebrew history but to reveal the hand of God in the affairs of men. According to Charles C. Cook, the books show how "the rise and splendor, and the decline and fall of the kingdom . . . were the results, respectively, of the piety and faithfulness, or the sin and idolatry of the various kings and their subjects. For this reason, much that would be of merely secular interest is omitted or summarized, while in-

12

cidents that deal particularly with the divine purpose, and the moral and religious conditions of rulers and people, are narrated at length."

## D. Importance of the Study of Kings and Chronicles

The study of these books is important because what they teach is contemporary and vital. Consider these points:

1. *Early history of an important nation.* This is the early history of an important nation—God's chosen people. The nation of Israel is in God's thought and purposes a key nation in the history of mankind. Israel's past, present, and future are most notable (cf. Rom. 9-11). In the past this nation was chosen by God to be His representative people: to receive, preserve, and pass on His communications to man. Through this nation we have our Bible. Through this nation our Lord and Saviour came when He took upon himself human form and dwelt among men. At present the Israelites, though scattered throughout the world, remain distinct among the people where they dwell; they are a constant witness of the truth and accuracy of the prophecies of Scripture. According to God's Word, this people has yet a great future upon the earth.

2. *A basic philosophy of history.* We may derive from Israel's history a basic philosophy of history. In God's dealings with this nation, we have a picture of His dealings with all nations and with all individuals, as far as the great principles of His activities are concerned. The books afford an inspired commentary on the affairs and destinies of men and nations under the ultimate and supreme Head, the Lord Himself.

In this part of Israel's history is repeatedly illustrated the truth stated in Daniel 4:25, 34-35: "The most High ruleth in the kingdom of men, and giveth it to whomsoever he will . . . whose dominion is an everlasting dominion, and his kingdom is from generation to generation: . . . and he doeth according to his will in the army of heaven, and among the inhabitants of the earth."

From the time of Adam until the present, all of God's dealings with men have been to induce them to trust Him and to prove their trust by obeying Him. God has given only one message to man from the beginning. The whole Bible is one message: *trust God.* Trust God for salvation. Trust God in the face of any danger or temptation. Trust God to supply every need. Trust God always, and trust God only, for the man who puts his trust in God shall never be ashamed. In Kings and Chronicles we continually see the wisdom of trusting and obeying God—and the disastrous results of failing to do so.

3. *Many spiritual lessons for Christian living.* In these books are recorded many prayers, warnings, and exhortations. Much is made of the Lord's mercy and of the help He offers His people. The justice of the Lord's judgments is made clear. The beauties of worship and praise appear again and again. Requirements for successful leadership are spelled out minutely. In your study of Kings and Chronicles be always alert to how the message applies to you personally. Remember, "the whole Bible was given to us by inspiration from God and is useful to teach us what is true and to make us realize what is wrong in our lives; it straightens us out and helps us do what is right. It is God's way of making us well-prepared at every point, fully equipped to do good to everyone" (2 Tim. 3:16-17, *The Living Bible*).

### E. Composition of the Books

In writing these books, the authors advantageously used the literary methods of selectivity (choosing what to include and what to exclude), condensation, and expansion. What the authors included, what they chose not to include, and the manner in which the books were written should be of interest to us. Let us look at Kings and Chronicles separately.

1. *Kings.* In these books the author seeks to give a rather comprehensive history of the leadership of all the tribes during this era. In 1 Kings 1-11 the narrative runs smoothly because only one kingdom (all the tribes of the united or undivided kingdom) is involved. From 1 Kings 12 to 2 Kings 17, however, with the two kingdoms (Israel—north, and Judah—south) existing side by side, the account reads with more difficulty, because the author has chosen to shift the narrative from the one kingdom to the other, in order to give simultaneous pictures. Then at 2 Kings 18 to the end, there is a return to the smooth flow again, since only the one surviving kingdom (Judah) is involved.

2. *Chronicles.* These books are more selective than Kings, illustrated in the fact that the northern kingdom of Israel is hardly mentioned. The author makes prominent the unbroken (though at times slender) thread of the covenant promise from the earliest days and through the Davidic dynasty, represented by the house of Judah (cf. 1 Chron. 28:4). Hence the inclusion of:

(a) The genealogies (1 Chron. 1-9), where the Davidic line, the descendants of Levi, and the two tribes of Judah and Benjamin are of chief interest

(b) The high points of Judah's history up to the captivity

(c) The prominent place given the Temple, priesthood, and other worship items

14

## F. The Setting of Kings and Chronicles

Just as the study of Judges is made easier by an acquaintance with the names of the various judges, so you will find it helpful in this early stage of your study of Kings and Chronicles to learn the names of the kings. Study the lists on pages 101 and 104, where the nineteen kings (plus one queen) of Judah and nineteen kings of Israel are listed chronologically. Some names appear in both groups but represent different men. Note the words "good" and "evil" designated for each king. It was part of the biblical writer's aim to issue a verdict on the character of the leadership of the kings. Keep these lists before you as you read Kings and Chronicles.

Next study the accompanying chart entitled *The Setting of Kings and Chronicles:*

1. Note the key historical *events* of this period:

| | | |
|---|---|---|
| 1043 B.C. | First king | |
| 931 B.C. | Division of the kingdom | |
| 722 B.C. | Fall of Samaria (northern kingdom) | |
| 586 B.C. | Fall of Jerusalem (southern kingdom) | |

2. Note where 1 Kings picks up the narrative. Note also that 2 Kings concludes at the fall of Jerusalem, but that it includes a brief epilogue (25:27) of a later date.

3. Note that 2 Kings picks up the narrative from 1 Kings at an uneventful junction. This confirms the approach to 1 and 2 Kings as *one* narrative.

4. Note that Elijah and Elisha are prominent characters in Kings. Look at the folded chart of Kings and Prophets and note that almost all of the prophets who lived after Elijah and Elisha were authors of prophetical books of the Bible. Why was the prophet's work so important for the kingdoms?

_____

_____

5. What three periods of kingdom history are covered by Kings?

_____

_____

6. Note the coverage of the books of Chronicles. Compare this with that of Kings. Does 2 Chronicles begin at an eventful junction?

Study this chart closely. If you master this visual aid, you will be helped immeasurably in your studies of Kings and Chronicles. One danger to guard against in the study of any history is to fail to

15

# THE SETTING OF KINGS AND CHRONICLES

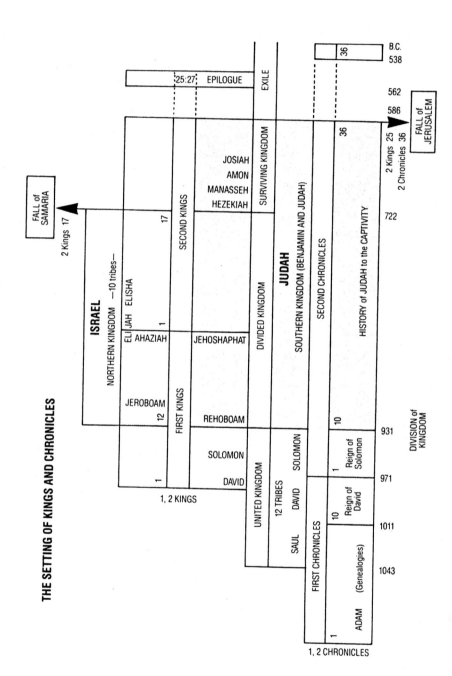

see the forest because of the host of trees. When you study Kings and Chronicles, keep before you this larger outline of the books as you analyze the smaller parts.

(Note: An exhaustive study of the setting of Kings and Chronicles would include a study of the prophetical books covering these years. Such a study is beyond the scope of this manual.)

## G. Plan of This Study Guide

The lessons of this study guide are organized around the outline of the first book of Kings. (The study guide that follows this one in the series covers 2 Kings.) Inasmuch as parts of Chronicles cover the same period, we shall at all times read and consider the parallel accounts of events given in Chronicles. Occasionally studies also will be made in passages unique to Chronicles.

Most of this study guide will emphasize the three things made prominent by the book of 1 Kings, which are:

1. The ministry of Solomon the king
2. The split of the kingdom
3. The ministry of Elijah the prophet

The accompanying diagram, anticipating the more complete survey chart of the next section, illustrates the above plan.

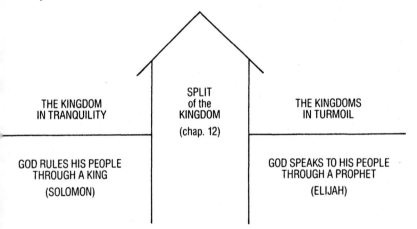

## H. Survey of 1 Kings

Read 1 Kings 22:37-53 and 2 Kings 1:1-4, and observe how the narrative of 1 Kings continues into 2 Kings without any significant break, indicating that the two books are virtually one unit.

Read all of 1 Kings at one sitting if possible. Record on the accompanying chart a segment title for each of the chapters (or parts of chapters) shown.

After you have finished this survey reading, answer these questions:

1. What impressed you about the book?

_____

2. What appeared to be some of the highlights?

_____

_____

3. How much action?

_____

How much description?

_____

How much conversation?

_____

4. Main characters?

_____

_____

Now study the accompanying survey chart, observing the following:

1. The book has twenty-two chapters; half of these concern the united kingdom and the other half concern the divided kingdom.
2. Observe where these events are recorded: David's death; the Temple chapters; Solomon's death; split of the northern tribes from Judah; the call and ministry of Elijah.
3. What do you consider to be key chapters in 1 Kings?

_____

4. Consider 9:4-5 as key verses for this book. In further studies you may find other verses that would serve as key verses. Note the title given to 1 Kings, as shown on the survey chart: "A Kingdom Divided Against Itself."
5. The book of 1 Kings covers about 130 years (971-841 B.C.). The first eleven chapters cover Solomon's reign of 40 years, and by adding the number of years that each of the other four kings in Judah reigned (see 14:21; 15:1-2; 15:8-10; 22:41-42), we arrive at the approximate time covered by the entire book.
6. Be sure to have a fair picture of the narrative of 1 Kings before you read the following section (The Story of 1 Kings), which summarizes its main contents.

# 1 KINGS   A KINGDOM DIVIDED AGAINST ITSELF

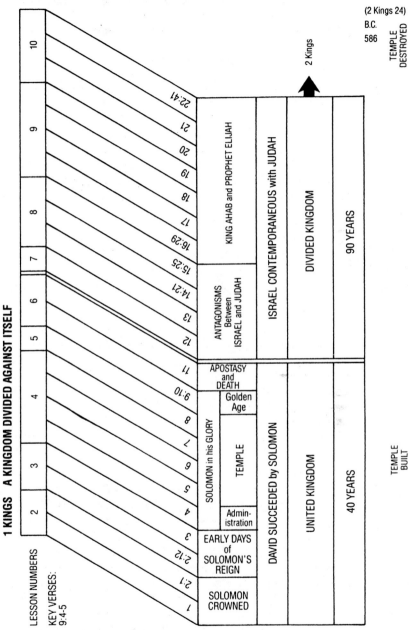

LESSON NUMBERS

| 2 | 3 | 4 | 5 | 6 | 7 | 8 | 9 | 10 |

KEY VERSES: 9:4-5

SOLOMON CROWNED — 1, 2:1

EARLY DAYS of SOLOMON'S REIGN — 2:12, 3

SOLOMON in his GLORY — Admin-istration (4), TEMPLE (5, 6, 7), Golden Age (8), 9:10

APOSTASY and DEATH — 11

ANTAGONISMS Between ISRAEL and JUDAH — 12, 13, 14:21, 15:25

KING AHAB and PROPHET ELIJAH — 16:29, 17, 18, 19, 20, 21, 22:41

DAVID SUCCEEDED by SOLOMON

ISRAEL CONTEMPORANEOUS with JUDAH

UNITED KINGDOM

DIVIDED KINGDOM

40 YEARS

90 YEARS

TEMPLE BUILT

2 Kings

(2 Kings 24)
B.C.
586
TEMPLE DESTROYED

19

## I. The Story of 1 Kings

In the first chapters of 1 Kings, Israel, as the nation of destiny, is seen to be at the very height of her power, prosperity, and influence. David's successful wars had greatly enlarged her borders and secured control over many of the nearby nations, such as Moab, Ammon, and Edom. Garrisons had been placed even as far as Damascus. (For the location of these places see map on page 7.)

The advantage thus established was maintained throughout the rule of Solomon. Although Solomon conducted no wars, his reign was marked by great internal development. He extended foreign commerce, executed great building schemes, increased the wealth, and advanced the culture of the nation. During Solomon's reign, the magnificence and the glory of his court excited the wonder and envy of all the surrounding nations.

Beginning with chapter 12, note a steady decline of the state of Israel, until, by the time 2 Kings completes the record, we see this once prosperous and powerful nation now poor and powerless, despised and in captivity—all because of sin.

Solomon, though exceedingly wise regarding many things, was most unwise in his disobedience to God's laws and his toleration of idolatry. Moreover, his excessive taxation of the people stirred up such discontent that shortly after his death ten of the twelve tribes of Israel revolted against the authority of Solomon's son Rehoboam and formed another kingdom in the northern part of the land, known thereafter as Israel. The two tribes that remained true to Solomon's son were known as Judah. (See map on page 7.) This was the beginning of the divided kingdom.

The ten-tribe kingdom of Israel was founded on idolatry (1 Kings 12:25-33), and things rapidly retrogressed from bad to worse. Before 1 Kings closes, Ahab's wicked queen, Jezebel, has made Baal worship the accepted religion of Israel; with Jezebel's wicked daughter Athaliah as queen on the throne of Judah, Baal worship saps the spiritual life of that kingdom also. What utter ruin the nation was headed for—all because they refused to acknowledge God as their king and obey Him!

The following outline of 1 Kings is given so that you may refer to it from time to time for orientation in your study.

Part I. THE UNITED KINGDOM (1:1–11:43)

    A. David (1:1–2:11)
        1. David makes Solomon king (1:1-53)
        2. David's charge to Solomon (2:1-9)
        3. David's death (2:10-11; cf. 1 Chron. 29:26-30)

B. Solomon (2:12–11:43)
   1. The beginning of Solomon's reign (2:12–3:28; cf. 2 Chron. 1:1-13)
   2. Solomon in all his glory (4:1–10:29; cf. 2 Chron. 1:14–9:28)
   3. Solomon's fall, chastisement, and death (chap. 11; cf. 2 Chron. 9:20-31)

Part II. THE DIVIDED KINGDOM (12:1–22:53)

(From the twelfth chapter to the end of the book, the kingdom of Judah and the kingdom of Israel are alternately in view. To indicate this the subheads are alternately designated "The Kingdom of Judah" and "The Kingdom of Israel," and the events under each of these are enumerated.)

A. The Kingdom of Judah (12:1-19)
   1. Accession and folly of Rehoboam (12:1-15; cf. 2 Chron. 10:1-11)
   2. Rebellion of the ten tribes (12:16-19; cf. 2 Chron. 10:12-19; 11:1-4)

B. The Kingdom of Israel (12:20–14:20)
   1. Accession and sin of Jeroboam (12:20-33)
   2. God's interposition (13:1-32)
   3. Jeroboam's continued sin and God's message (13:33–14:18)
   4. Jeroboam's death (14:19-20)

C. The Kingdom of Judah (14:21–15:24)
   1. Judah's sin and idolatry (14:21-24; 2 Chron. 12:1)
   2. God's chastisement and mercy (14:25-30; 2 Chron. 12:2-12)
   3. Death of Rehoboam (14:31; 2 Chron. 12:13-16)
   4. Abijam (15:1-8; 2 Chron. 13:1-2)
   5. Asa (15:9-24; 2 Chron. 14:1; 16:1-6, 12-14)

D. The Kingdom of Israel (15:25–22:40)
   1. Nadab (15:25-26)
   2. Baasha (15:27-34)
   3. God's message (16:1-7)
   4. Elah (16:8-10)
   5. Zimri (16:10-20)
   6. Omri (16:21-28)
   7. Ahab (16:29–22:40)

E. The Kingdom of Judah (22:41-50)
Jehoshaphat (22:41-50; 2 Chron. 17:1–20:31)

F. The Kingdom of Israel (22:51-53)
Ahaziah (22:51-53)

### J. Prepare to Analyze

In preparing to analyze the smaller individual parts of 1 Kings, follow these suggestions:

1. Review the place of the kingdoms in Israel's history.

2. Review the historical setting of Kings and Chronicles (chart of page 16).

3. Review these relationships of Kings and Chronicles: (1) to each other, (2) to the books of Samuel, (3) to Ezra, and (4) to the books of the prophets (e.g., Jeremiah).

4. Keep in mind the functions of priests, prophets, and kings, as God desired these men to minister to His people.

5. Keep in mind the general structure (survey chart page 19) of 1 Kings.

6. Study with the strong desire to let God, through His Holy Spirit, teach you from His Word. Be willing to devote much time to your study. Do not let activities of lesser importance crowd out your personal Bible study.

# Solomon Crowned

T he story of these chapters concerns the last major ministries of
David as king of Israel, as he rescued the throne for Solomon
from a would-be usurper and gave a charge to his successor Solomon and the people to follow after the Lord.

Look at the chart on page 16 and recall that the events of the
last days of David are recorded in the last part of 1 Chronicles and
the first part of 1 Kings.

Note: The name *Israel* in the Bible sometimes refers to the
entire nation and sometimes only to the northern kingdom of the
ten tribes. In this study guide the name refers to the entire nation
when the period of the united kingdom is involved, and to the
northern tribes during the divided kingdom years. (Exceptions to
this will be so stated.) Which kingdom period do the chapters of
this lesson concern?

## I. ANALYSIS

First read 1 Chronicles 29:22, observing that there were two
coronations of Solomon. Recall that both Saul and David had ex-
perienced a double coronation—the second being a public confirmation of the first (1 Sam. 10:1; 11:15; 2 Sam. 2:4; 5:3).

Read 1 Kings 1:1–2:11 and 1 Chronicles 28-29, in that order,
to gain an overall view of the passage and some impressions of
the prominent items.

For your second reading, observe the paragraph divisions
shown of the accompanying charts. Record paragraph titles for
each paragraph. Try to determine for yourself groupings of paragraphs according to subject matter. Record these. Then study the
accompanying outlines. Proceed from this point in your analysis
to other observations. *Keep looking* at the Bible text. Record ob-

## 1 KINGS 1:1—2:11

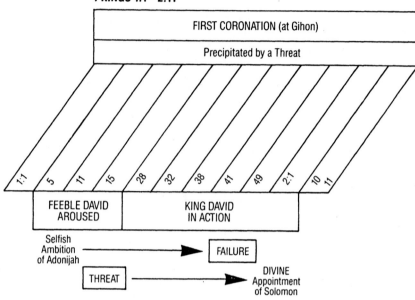

FIRST CORONATION (at Gihon)

Precipitated by a Threat

| 1:1 | 5 | 11 | 15 | 28 | 32 | 38 | 41 | 49 | 2:1 | 10 | 11 |

FEEBLE DAVID AROUSED

KING DAVID IN ACTION

Selfish Ambition of Adonijah ⟶ FAILURE

THREAT ⟶ DIVINE Appointment of Solomon

## 1 CHRONICLES 28-29

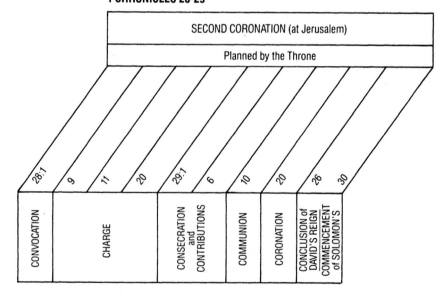

SECOND CORONATION (at Jerusalem)

Planned by the Throne

| 28:1 | 9 | 11 | 20 | 29:1 | 6 | 10 | 20 | 26 | 30 |

CONVOCATION

CHARGE

CONSECRATION and CONTRIBUTIONS

COMMUNION

CORONATION

CONCLUSION of DAVID'S REIGN

COMMENCEMENT of SOLOMON'S

24

servations in your Bible and on paper as you proceed. Throughout this manual you will be constantly urged to *look* and *record*. These are two of the most important requirements for profitable Bible study.

1. Which of the two coronations was more elaborate and impressive?

---

FIRST CORONATION (1 Kings 1:1–2:11)

2. What was the purpose of the author in prefacing the story of Adonijah with 1:1-4?

---

(Note: Concerning this strange practice, "the suggestion of the servants that a maiden be found for the king to restore his lost vitality and to provide him warmth was an accepted medical prescription even down to the Middle Ages."[1] About how old was David at this time? (Cf. 2 Sam. 5:4)

---

3. Read 1:5-10. Who were Adonijah, Abiathar, and Joab?

---

Compare Adonijah's "I will be king" with 1 Chronicles 28:5. Explain why Solomon was not invited to the feast.

---

4. Compare the feeble David of 1:1 with the aroused David of 1:28ff.

---

5. Compare the atmosphere of 1:38-40 with that of 1:41-50. Explain the difference.

---

6. What good qualities of Solomon are revealed in 1:52-53?

---

1. Charles F. Pfeiffer and Everett F. Harrison, eds., *The Wycliffe Bible Commentary* (Chicago: Moody Press, 1962), p. 309.

7. Read 2:1-9. The first four verses record general exhortations of David's charge; the remaining verses record specific instructions. Analyze carefully the first part. Notice David's appeal to continuity.

SECOND CORONATION (1 Chron. 28:1–29:30)
8. Read 28:1-8. Note how representative was the company assembled at Jerusalem for this auspicious ceremony. What is the key word of verses 4-7?

_____

How is Daniel 4:17, 24-25 demonstrated here?

_____

Complete the following, concerning the progressively narrowing choice (also read the references):

| From this: | God chose: | Reference: |
|---|---|---|
| 12 sons of Jacob | _____ | Gen. 49:8-10 |
| tribe of Judah | _____ | 1 Sam. 16:1 |
| sons of Jesse | _____ | 1 Sam. 16:6-13 |
| sons of David | _____ | 1 Chron. 29:5 |

9. What is the significance of David's words "the throne of the kingdom of the Lord over Israel" (28:5)?

_____

10. Read 28:9-10. Identify the commands.

_____

_____

Identify the conditions.

_____

_____

Identify the statements of fact.

_____

_____

Compare this charge with 28:7 and 1 Kings 2:1-4. How does this charge apply to Christian living today?

_____

_____

26

11. Read 28:11-19. Where did David get the plans and specifications (patterns) for the Temple?

Read Exodus 25:40 for the source of the plans for the Tabernacle. Why did God specify such and elaborate and expensive temple?

Of which temptation to sin would the people have to be especially cautious?

Apply this to the church today.

12. Read 28:20-21. Compare David's words with those of Moses to Joshua (Deut. 31:6-8) and of God to Joshua (Josh. 1:6-7).

13. Read 29:1-9. Note David's example of giving and the lever it afforded to make an appeal to others. What was David appealing to in the hearts of the people?

Did he succeed?

Account for the joy of verse 9.

Read 2 Corinthians 8:12; 9:7. Truly, when the *heart* is right, the *purse* is opened for the work of God.

14. Read 29:10-19. Analyze carefully David's prayer of thanksgiving and praise. There are three parts to the prayer: 29:10-13; 14-16; 17-19.

Write a title for each part. What is the key word of the third part?

List some important lessons on prayer taught by this segment.

15. Read 29:20-25. What elements of splendor and glory appear here?

_____

_____

Explain verse 25.

_____

Why did Zadok (v. 22) replace Abiathar? (Cf. 1 Kings 1:7; 2:26)

_____

16. List some of the major spiritual lessons taught by these chapters in such areas as the ways of God, Christian living, and the ministry of leadership.

_____

_____

_____

_____

## II. COMMENTS

David was the greatest and the best of all the human kings who ever ruled over God's earthly people, Israel. David always acknowledged his proper position, one subordinate to his Maker. While he sat on an earthly throne, he never lost sight of the throne in heaven. He never forgot that Israel's *true* king was Jehovah. He was a man after God's own heart. David was not sinless, but when he sinned he repented and turned from his sin. He willed to do God's will, rather than his own. Although he sometimes fell under temptation, he habitually worshiped and served God rather than self. To the very end of his career, his chief concern was for God's work, God's Word, and God's glory. In his attitude toward God, David was in great contrast to most of the kings who succeeded him.

### A. The Coronations of Solomon

The occasion for David's making Solomon king the first time was Adonijah's plot to seize the kingdom. At that time Adonijah was the eldest of David's living sins. He was good-looking and sufficiently popular to win over Joab, the military leader of the nation, and Abiathar, the priest and religious leader, to his cause.

No doubt Adonijah knew that David intended to make Solomon his successor. This was probably the reason that Solomon was the only son of David who was not invited to the feast held in honor of Adonijah's proclamation.

But One greater than David had chosen Solomon to be king; God Himself had appointed him. No plans of man could change that decree. When Solomon was born, God loved him and sent Nathan the prophet to say that he should be called Jedidiah, meaning "beloved of the Lord" (see 2 Sam. 12:24-25). And now, through the planning of this same prophet, Nathan, David was informed of Adonijah's plot (1 Kings 1:10-27).

Knowledge of the plot aroused something of the aged monarch's former vigor and determination. Sharply and decisively he gave orders: "Call me Bathsheba. . . . Call me Zadok the priest, and Nathan the prophet, . . . cause Solomon my son to ride upon mine own mule, . . . anoint him . . . king over Israel" (1 Kings 1:28-35).

The prompt carrying out of these commands won over the whole nation to the cause of David and Solomon. Even Adonijah and his fellow conspirators at last submitted to Solomon and acknowledged him king of Israel. The second coronation of Solomon, a confirmation of the first, was a pageant of splendor and majesty. David had summoned all the heads of his well-organized kingdom to hear his final counsel and commands. Multitudes of the people were in attendance as well. The parties involved in the ceremony were:

David—The retiring king
Solomon—The new king
Rulers and people—The constituency of the kingdom
The Lord—The King

A noteworthy aspect of this event was the spirit of David. David was careful to give the Lord the prominent place in the things said and done. He might have used this last great occasion of his public career to exalt himself, for he had an enviable record. He might have said more about his son Solomon. Instead the spotlight of attention was directed to the Lord and to the demands of His kingship.

At the end of the ceremony David said to the people, "Now bless the Lord your God!" (1 Chron. 29:20). And all the congregation blessed the Lord God of their fathers. There was praise, there was obedience, and there was commitment to walk in the way of the Lord.

## B. The Death of David

And David died "in a good old age (at least seventy), full of days, riches, and honour" (1 Chron. 29:28). Much meaning is packed into that sentence. The riches were spiritual as well as material. The honor was of God as well as of men.

See the statement made in 1 Kings 2:10: "So David slept with his fathers, and was buried in the city of David."

H. J. Carpenter writes, "Other kings great and wise and good were to succeed him, but of no other was it said that Jerusalem was *their* city. No small honor to be the founder of a city that was destined to be one day the city of which the Messiah Himself would come with sovereign claims. No small honor to be made a model king against whose righteous government the reigns of other kings were set in contrast for praise or blame, according as they did, or did not, as David their father."

## III. SUMMARY

As a concluding exercise, read 1 Chronicles 29:22-28 again, observing how the verses serve as a summary of these events. Note the following sequence:

| | |
|---|---|
| BEGINNING OF A REIGN | "And they made Solomon the son of David king . . ." |
| HERITAGE OF THE PREDECESSOR | "Then Solomon sat on the throne . . . in the place of David" |
| OBEDIENCE OF THE FOLLOWERS | "And all Israel obeyed him. And all the princes, . . . mighty men, . . . sons of King David, submitted themselves unto Solomon" |
| BLESSING OF GOD | "And the Lord magnified Solomon" |
| END OF A REIGN | "And David . . . died" |

# Lesson 3

# Early Days of Solomon's Reign

In the previous lesson we learned more about David than about Solomon, even though Solomon's coronations were the main subjects. The reason for this is that the purpose of these chapters is to emphasize David's part in the coronations.

With this lesson we begin the study of King Solomon's reign. Look at the chart on page 16 and note that the account of his reign extends to the end of chapter 11 of 1 Kings, which records the close of the united kingdom. Then look at the survey chart on page 19 and note that 1 Kings records four phases of Solomon's reign: Solomon crowned, early days of Solomon's reign, Solomon in his glory, and Solomon's apostasy and death. The second of these is the subject of this lesson.

## I. ANALYSIS

Before you read the text of 1 Kings, mark in your Bible the following outline according to the divisions shown:

A. Removal of Adversaries
   1. Adonijah 2:13-25
   2. Abiathar 2:26-27
   3. Joab 2:28-35
   4. Shimei 2:36-46

B. Marriage and Sacrifices 3:1-4 (2 Chron. 1:2-6)

C. Dream, Prayer and Demonstration 3:5-28 (2 Chron. 1:7-13)

   Now read through the passage in one sitting, keeping in mind the above outline. Write down some of your impressions of the basis of this reading. Return to the text, including the Chronicles passages, looking especially for what it teaches about Solo-

31

|  | WHAT IS LEARNED ABOUT SOLOMON? | WHAT IS LEARNED ABOUT GOD? |
|---|---|---|
| **Removal of Adversaries** (2:13-46) | | |
| **Marriage and Sacrifice** (3:1-4) (2 Chron. 1:2-6) | | |
| **Dreams, Prayer & Demonstration** (3:5-28) (2 Chron. 1:7-13) | | |

mon and about God. Record these items in the accompanying chart.

## II. COMMENTS

Solomon's reign began auspiciously. He occupied the position of his honored father. The whole nation had received him as their monarch, and his kingdom was firmly established. Solomon's authority seems to have been absolute (1 Chron. 29:23-25).

Note that Solomon's throne is referred to in 1 Kings 2:12 as "the throne of David," whereas in 1 Chronicles 29:23 as "the throne of the Lord." As was pointed out earlier, 1 and 2 Kings give the history from the *human* point of view; 1 and 2 Chronicles from the *divine* standpoint. Constantly we are reminded that "the kingdom is the Lord's."

### A. Removal of Adversaries

The account of Solomon's removal of his adversaries brings before us four influential men who were banished, that is, Adonijah, Solomon's elder brother; Abiathar, the priest; Joab, the military leader; and Shimei, a wealthy, crafty prince.

1. *Adonijah.* Adonijah's crime was his second plot to gain the throne. Thus Solomon interpreted Adonijah's request to marry Abishag. Abishag was a member of the royal household, considered as David's daughter or secondary wife. According to Eastern standards, one who was a member of the royal household was recognized as one who stood near succession to the throne. Adonijah, having failed to gain the throne by force, apparently was seeking it by craft; to wed Abishag was the first step toward realizing his ambition. Bathsheba was completely deceived by Adonijah's plausible arguments and his religious attitude, but Solomon saw clearly through his mask and perceived that he was aiming at the throne. From Solomon's mention of Abiathar and Joab in connection with Adonijah's request, it is to be inferred that they were plotting with Adonijah in this matter, even as they had been associated with his first attempt to become king.

2. *Abiathar.* Abiathar was removed from the priesthood because he was associated with Adonijah in the conspiracy against Solomon. Treason was punishable by death. But because of Solomon's respect for the office of the priesthood and because of Abiathar's past service under King David (cf. 2 Sam. 15:24ff.), Solomon merely removed him from being priest and put Zadok in his place.

Notice that Abiathar was removed from his office because of his own acts. He richly deserved his fate. However, notice also that his removal fulfilled a prophecy of God against the house of Eli (1 Kings 2:27; cf. 1 Sam. 2:30-33). Abiathar was descended from Eli. Every prophecy of God is sure to be fulfilled, whether the fulfillment comes in the near future or in the far distant future.

3. *Joab*. The execution of Joab and Shimei was the carrying out of one of David's last injunctions to Solomon. Joab was guilty of treason and murder, and it was for murder that he was put to death (cf. 2 Sam. 3:27-29). Notice that the man who acted as Joab's executioner was placed at the head of the army, the position that Joab had so long occupied.

4. *Shimei*. Shimei was probably the only remaining representative of the house of Saul. He deserved death because of his treatment of God's anointed king (2 Sam. 16:5-80). David had charged Solomon, "His hoar head bring thou down to the grave with blood"; but the further and immediate reason for his being put to death was that he had not kept the oath of the Lord and had disobeyed the commandment of the king (1 Kings 2:42-43, 46).

The conspirators were thus all removed. It was a remarkable feat of Solomon to gain complete hold of the reins of government at so young an age (around twenty).

### B. Marriage and Sacrifices

1. *Solomon's wife*. His wife is not identified by name. This marriage was a political move, as seen by the phrase "Solomon made affinity [alliance] with Pharaoh" (3:1). A peaceful relationship with Egypt was thus nurtured. If Pharaoh's daughter was a pagan when Solomon took her as his wife, then he was breaking the commandment of Exodus 34:16. Though the text here does not rebuke this marriage union, the verses of 1 Kings 11:1-8 place this marriage along with the other evil ones. It is clear from the study of Solomon's life that his marriage "alliances" were primary causes of his eventual undoing. If Pharaoh's daughter consented to become a proselyte to the Jewish religion, she nevertheless hindered Solomon from remaining true to God.

2. *High places*. The term "high places" originated with the Canaanite religions, in which cultic objects on elevated platforms were worshiped. During the period of the judges and pre-Temple years of Solomon's reign, the Israelites carried over the setting of "high places" into their own worship ceremonies, though they dedicated such places to Jehovah God. Having many "high places" obviously dulled the people's anticipation of a *central* sanctuary, such as that described in Deuteronomy 12:11-14. The only two le-

gitimate places for divine sacrifice at this time were Gibeon, where the Tabernacle of the Lord was (2 Chron. 1:3) and Jerusalem, where the Ark of God was (2 Chron. 1:4). Solomon sinned in not observing this.

Even after the Temple was built, and during the days of the kings that succeeded Solomon, worship at the "high places" continued to defile the nation of God (cf. 1 Kings 12:25-33).

### C. Dream, Prayer, and Demonstration

One night after Solomon's great sacrifice and while he was yet at Gibeon, God appeared to him in a dream and told him to pray for the gift he most desired. In Solomon's prayer we observe that the first note is that of praise and the next of unselfish petition. He desired the gift of wisdom, not for selfish reasons but that it might be used for the benefit of his people and to the glory of his God. Read Ephesians 3:20 in the light of 1 Kings 3:12-13.

God *unconditionally* gave Solomon the gifts of wisdom, wealth, and honor. But the gift of prolonged life was offered to him on the *condition* that he should keep God's statutes and commandments as David had done. In view of Solomon's failing to fulfill this condition in later years, his death at age sixty may be viewed as premature. Solomon was probably about eighteen or twenty when he began to reign, and he reigned forty years. His words "I am but a little child" (1 Kings 3:7) refer not only to his youth but to his lack of experience.

Solomon's judgment concerning the two harlots was public demonstration to all Israel that "a superhuman discernment had taken up its home within him." Israel was convinced that he had a God-given power to detect wrong and discern truth and falsehood.

### III. SUMMARY

These chapters relate Solomon's discharge of royal functions in four major areas:

1. internal threats (removal of adversaries)
2. international alliances (marriage)
3. worship of God (sacrifices)
4. rule of the people (prayer for understanding)

Solomon's rule was not flawless during his young years. If he could nip in the bud those sins that would so quickly beget bigger sins, then there was every prospect of a bright and flourishing era ahead for Israel. The construction of the magnificent Temple (the subject of our next lesson) was a token of glory that might have pervaded the entire life of Israel.

# Lesson 4

Lesson 4      *1 Kings 5:1–7:51*
*2 Chronicles 2:1–4:22*

# Construction of the Temple

The Temple is a key item in the narrative of Kings: 1 Kings records its construction, whereas 2 Kings records its destruction (380 years later). More than one-third of that space of 1 Kings devoted to the reign of Solomon speaks about the Temple.

Why did the Temple play such an important part in the life of Israel? One good answer is found in the purpose of the Temple's predecessor, the portable Tabernacle. God revealed much about Himself and His work of redemption to His people through the symbols of the Tabernacle. One important truth was that He should be *the* center of the life of Israel, and Him only should Israel worship and serve. In the timetable of Israel it was appropriate and necessary that a permanent temple now be set up to replace the Tabernacle. David had wanted to build this temple, but his commission involved more of the military in order to rid the land of many of Israel's enemies. Now that the kingdom had been extended and there was internal unity and external peace, the time had come for Solomon to erect the building. (Read 2 Sam. 7:11-13.)

## I. ANALYSIS

### A. Solomon's Administration (1 Kings 4:1-34; 2 Chron. 1:14-17)

Before recording the story about the Temple, the author of 1 Kings describes something of the organization and size of Solomon's kingdom and remarks on the wisdom he exercised in governing that kingdom.

First read 2 Chronicles 1:14-17. Then read 1 Kings 4, observing the following paragraph divisions and recording the main content of each of them:

4:1-6
_____

7-19
_____

20-25
_____

26-28
_____

29-34
_____

This is a chapter of *big* things. Check each paragraph again, noting the theme of bigness running throughout the chapter. Is bigness necessarily a sign of goodness? Now follow these study questions:
1. Compare the first and last verses. What is the significance of the word "all"?

_____

2. Read 4:20-25. Do these verses intend to describe the material or the spiritual prosperity of Solomon's kingdom?

_____

Note: Verse 20*b* reads thus in the Berkeley Version: "They ate, drank and enjoyed life." The footnote explains that these words are "not intimating that the people thought of nothing else, but that, enjoying divine blessing, they were happy and content."

Study the map on page 7, showing the extent of Solomon's kingdom. Notice the locations of the Euphrates River ("the river" of 4:1, 24), Tiphsah, Azzah (Gaza), Dan, and Beersheba.
3. Read 4:29-34. By what different ways is Solomon's wisdom measured here?

_____

_____

What type of wisdom is described?

_____

Does this wisdom guarantee spiritual well-being?

_____

The extent of Solomon's domination was far-reaching: from the Euphrates River in the east and north to the border of Egypt in the west and south. This may have represented as much as 50,000 square miles. "It might seem impossible . . . with two such strong contending powers as Egypt to the south and Assyria to the north . . . to build so large an empire, but such was the case at the beginning of Solomon's reign. At this time, the kingdom of Egypt was ruled by the weak and inglorious Twenty-first Dynasty; and the power of Assyria was in a state of decline."[1]

Solomon was an expert in such fields of knowledge as botany and zoology. God used this to His own glory when He inspired Solomon to write books like Proverbs, in which spiritual truths are illustrated by the pictures afforded by the physical world. Read some of Proverbs, keeping this background in mind. (It should be noted here that Solomon's biblical writings—Proverbs, Ecclesiastes, Song of Solomon, and at least two psalms (72, 127)—constituted an important part of his ministry, even overshadowing, in the perspective of the ages, the part he played in building the Temple.)

The large budget of Solomon's kingdom demanded heavy taxation for a time, but later on it was one of the chief causes for the rebellion of the ten tribes (chapter 12).

**B. Construction of the Temple** (1 Kings 5:1–7:51; 2 Chron. 2:1–4:22)

First, read 2 Chronicles 2:1 and 3:1 and observe these two aspects of the Temple project:

Preparation for building ("Solomon determined to build a house," 2 Chron. 2:1)

Building and furnishing ("Then Solomon began to build," 2 Chron. 3:1)

You will find similar statements in 1 Kings 5:5 and 1 Kings 6:1.

*Preparation for building* (1 Kings 5:1-18; 2 Chron. 2:1-18). (Paragraphs: 1 Kings 5:1-6; 7-12; 13-18; 2 Chron. 2:1-10; 11-16; 17-18.) Read the texts of both books, and then answer the following questions:

1. From what the text reveals, how important was the Temple project in Solomon's view?

_____

2. What part had David already played in preparations for the building of God's house? Read 1 Chronicles 29:1-9.

3. When did Solomon begin to build the Temple? (6:1)

_____

1. Charles F. Pfeiffer and Everett F. Harrison, eds., *The Wycliffe Bible Commentary* (Chicago: Moody, 1962), p. 314.

How long a time may he have been engaged in the preparation stage?

_____

4. Is there anything in the text to indicate whether King Hiram and the chief engraver were believers? (1 Kings 7:13-14; 2 Chron. 2:13-14)

_____

_____

Compare this situation with that of the building of the Tabernacle in the wilderness, where none but Israelites were the builders.

_____

_____

5. What attitude of heart is revealed in 2 Chronicles 2:5-6?

_____

_____

*Buildings and furnishings* (1 Kings 6-7; 2 Chron. 3-4). First read the Kings passage, recording the main content of each of the following units in the space provided.
6:1-10

_____

11-13

_____

14-22

_____

23-28

_____

29-36

_____

37-38

_____

7:1-8

_____

9-12

_____

13-14

---

15-22

---

23-26

---

27-37

---

38-40*a*

---

40*b*-50

---

51

---

Read the Chronicles passage, noting any major additions to the description.

1. What are your impressions of the Temple and its construction in regard to such things as size, cost, adornments, etc.? Compare 2 Chronicles 2:9 (KJV's "wonderful great" reads "great and marvelous" in the Berkeley Version).

---

---

2. The Lord's words of 1 Kings 6:12-13 were spoken to Solomon while the building was under construction. Why did the Lord confirm the covenant conditions at this time?

---

What spiritual dangers would threaten Solomon and the people at such a time as this?

---

---

3. What is emphasized in the paragraph 2 Chronicles 4:19-22?

---

---

What spiritual truth is taught here?

---

---

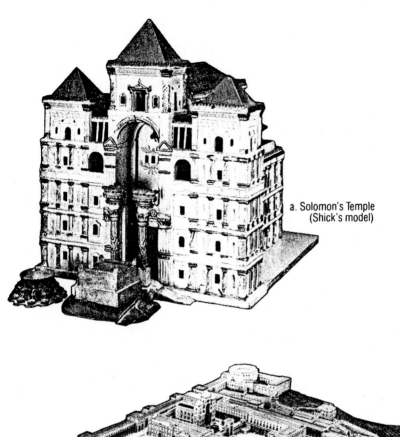

a. Solomon's Temple
(Shick's model)

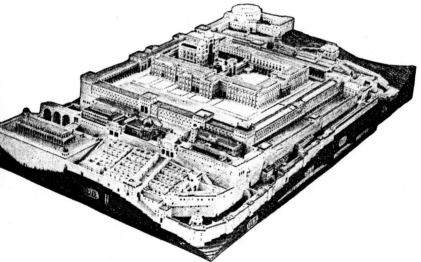

b. The temple with its associated annex buildings and court areas
(Shick's model)

Matson Photo Service

41

4. Refer to a Bible encyclopedia or dictionary for a concise description of the Temple. Study the photographs on page 41 of Solomon's Temple, the Temple area, and other associated buildings. Identify in photo (b) the actual Temple building. Reread the biblical text and try to visualize the buildings and areas.

5. If you are interested in making a thorough study of these chapters, you should consult commentaries for help on the more difficult parts of the text.

6. Write out a list of spiritual lessons that may be learned from these chapters. Most of your applications will probably come from these two areas:

    (a) words and actions of the narrative

    (b) symbols (especially the *major* items of the Temple)

Among other things, apply these chapters to present-day building programs of local churches.

---

---

---

## II. COMMENTS

In the early years of Solomon's reign the absorbing interest of his life was the building of the Temple.

Almost immediately after he became king, Solomon must have begun the extensive preparations recorded in chapter 5 of 1 Kings. His negotiations with the king of Tyre (vv. 1-12), the raising of the levy of 30,000 men (v. 13), the detailed organization of the work (vv. 14-16), the preparation of the material, and the bringing of it to the site of the Temple (vv. 17-18) must have occupied at least three years, for we read in 1 Kings 6:1 that in the fourth year of Solomon's reign the actual erection of the structure was begun.

It must not be forgotten that David also had made great preparations for the building of the house of the Lord (1 Chron. 29:2). Before his death he had in readiness much of the gold, silver, precious stones and marble that were to be used.

What David had prepared had been given willingly (1 Chron. 29:6-9). What Solomon prepared was done by hired labor (1 Kings 5:6), or forced labor (1 Kings 5:13-17). The 30,000 men mentioned in 1 Kings 5:13 were Israelites whose labor was compulsory until their period of service was completed. The workmen mentioned in 1 Kings 5:15 and 2 Chronicles 2:2 were not Israelites but Canaanites whom Solomon had made permanent

42

slaves, as can be seen by comparing 2 Chronicles 2:17-18 and 1 Kings 9:20-21.

The 3,000 thousand "overseers" mentioned in 2 Chronicles 2:18 and 1 Kings 5:16 "ruled over the people that wrought in the work," suggesting a picture of servitude such as the Israelites had known in Egypt.

The chief engraver, who worked in the gold and silver and brass (2 Chron. 2:12-14), was a man of mixed blood, his mother being an Israelite of the tribe of Dan who had married a man of Tyre (1 Kings 7:14).

King Hiram of Tyre, with whom Solomon made a league, may not have been a worshiper of God. He recognized God as the Maker of heaven and earth and as the God of Israel (e.g., 2 Chron. 2:12), but nothing recorded in the text reveals to us that the Lord was his own personal God. Another interesting observation to be made about the Temple's construction is that Gentiles had much to do with its building, whereas only Israelites built the wilderness Tabernacle.

Solomon realized something of the importance of this building he was about to erect and also something of his own insignificance (2 Chron. 2:4-6). The Temple was to be not only a central place of worship but the actual dwelling place of almighty God. No wonder Solomon said it should be "great and marvelous," even as David had said: "The house that is to be builded for the Lord must be exceeding magnificent, of fame and of glory throughout all countries" (1 Chron. 22:5).

Some of the prominent features of the Temple, including its size, layout, furniture, and associated buildings, are noted below.

1. The erection of the Temple was begun 966 B.C., in the fourth year of Solomon's reign, 480 years after the exodus from Egypt. The Temple took seven years to build. This was a comparatively short time for such a spectacular work, but, as *The Wycliffe Bible Commentary* points out: (1) much of the preparation had been completed beforehand; (2) the building was relatively small, though ornate; (3) a huge personnel was employed in the task.

2. The pattern for this building had been given David by the Lord (1 Chron. 28:19), and David had given the pattern to Solomon (1 Chron. 28:11-12; 2 Chron. 3:3). This divine blueprint is not contradicted by its similarities to Phoenician architecture of that day.

3. The Temple was similar to the Tabernacle in its overall layout. Both Temple and Tabernacle had two prominent areas known as the "holy place" and the "most holy place," or "holy of holies." In the text of Kings and Chronicles these areas are called by the following names:

|  | 1 Kings 6:27, 20 | 2 Chronicles 3:5, 8 |
|---|---|---|
| the holy place | "the house" | "the greater house" |
| the most holy place | "the oracle" | "the most holy house" |

Some differences between the Temple and the Tabernacle are as follows:

| Tabernacle | Temple |
|---|---|
| Length: 45'<br>Width: 15'<br>Height: 15' | Length: 90'<br>Width: 30'<br>Height: 45' |
| no porch | a porch in front (1 Kings 6:2-3): 30' long |
| Most Holy Place contained only the Ark of the Covenant | Two cherubim above the Ark (1 Kings 6:23-28) (not to be confused with the cherubim **on** the Ark) and the Ark (2 Chron. 5:7-8) in this room |
| no light transits | windows of narrow lights (1 Kings 6:4) in the Holy Place |
| veil separated the Holy Place from the Most Holy Place | veil (2 Chron 3:14) and doors separated the two rooms (1 Kings 6:31-32) |

4. The Temple was built of stone, lined with cedar, and overlaid with gold. The interior of the Temple was exceedingly beautiful, adorned with carvings and precious stones.

5. The two pillars placed before the Temple were called Jachin ("He shall establish") and Boaz ("In Him is strength"). Read Jeremiah's words concerning these pillars (Jer. 27:19-22) and the fulfillment of his words (2 Kings 25:13-17).

6. The pieces of furniture of "the vessels that pertained to the house of the Lord" (1 Kings 7:48) were similar to those used in the Tabernacle, but there was a difference in size and number. In the Tabernacle there was but one laver, one candlestick, and one table of showbread. All the vessels mentioned for the Temple were made on a much larger scale and were greater in number than those of the Tabernacle. Note the size of the brazen altar (2 Chron. 4:1); also note the description of the molten sea (2 Chron. 4:2-5).

7. Although Solomon made a new brazen altar, new candlesticks, tables, lavers, pots, shovels, and fleshhooks for the Temple, he did not make a new Ark of the Covenant. The Ark that was

brought into the Temple was the one that had been made at Mount Sinai. Explain this.

8. Solomon's own house consisted of various houses or halls (1 Kings 7:1-12): the House of the Forest of Lebanon (so called because its cedars came from Lebanon); the Hall of Pillars; the Hall of the Throne (Hall of Judgment); his personal royal court; and a palace for his wife.

## III. CONCLUSION

The Temple was the first large single structure undertaken by any Israelite ruler. Great as was Solomon's task in overseeing the construction of the Temple, his greater responsibility was his spiritual leadership of the people. God said that His dwelling among the children of Israel depended upon Solomon's faithfulness. But Solomon, great and wise as he was, failed in his faithfulness to God, and the idolatry that he later introduced caused the whole nation to be unfaithful to God.

# Dedication of the Temple

About eleven months after the Temple was completed, Solomon called his people together for a service of dedication. This house was built for the Lord, and Solomon wanted the dedication ceremony to be as impressive as the object to be dedicated. Your study of these chapters will reveal how successful he was.

The activities held in connection with the dedication lasted a little more than two weeks. First was a week of dedication feast; this was followed immediately by the Feast of Tabernacles, lasting one week; then the people were sent home (see 1 Kings 8:65-66). As you read the chapters of this lesson, visualize as much as possible the setting and action.

The biblical text does not record any one moment of dedicatory rite during the course of the days. The verse 8:63*b* has the connotation of the *general* time of dedication (e.g., see Berkeley Version). In a sense the dedication was composed of *many* ingredients, such as prayer, actions, appeals, promises, and God's response. This suggests many important truths taught by these chapters.

## I. ANALYSIS

Before reading the text, study carefully the following outline. Then mark the divisions in your Bible, as a help in keeping the "whole" in mind as you study the parts.

After you have read the 1 Kings passage once, read 2 Chronicles 5-7. Note places where Chronicles gives additional information; then go back to Kings and note what few parts are unique to that book (e.g., 2 Chron. 5:12-14; 6:13; 40-42; 7:1-3, 6, 14-16; 1 Kings 8:50*b*-61).

## A. Preparation (1 Kings 8:1-11)

Identify the main actors:

_____

_____

Identify the various actions:

_____

_____

What are some of the *key words* of this paragraph?

_____

In view of Israel's history up to that point, what was the spiritual significance surrounding each of the following:
ark

_____

covenant

_____

tabernacle

_____

sacrifice

_____

two tables of stone

_____

cloud

_____

## B. Address (1 Kings 8:12-21)

Whom is Solomon addressing?

_____

What is his main point?

_____

What is implied by the statement "The Lord said that he would dwell in the thick darkness"?

_____

How does the context help interpret this?

_____

## C. Prayer (1 Kings 8:22-53)

Notice the repeated word "hearken" (or "hear"). After the ascription of praise (8:23-24), a series of requests is made. List these in the following spaces.

25-30

_____

31-32

_____

33-34

_____

35-36

_____

37-40

_____

41-43

_____

44-45

_____

46-53

_____

Now write a list of the spiritual lessons taught here about prayer itself and about such related subjects as contriteness of heart, confession, forgiveness, dependency on God, justice of God, sin, and the all-seeing eye of God.

_____

_____

_____

_____

_____

Study carefully 8:41-43. What is taught here about the universality of the message of salvation?

_____

What "temple truths" are taught in the following New Testament verses: 1 Corinthians 3:16; 2 Corinthians 6:16; Revelation 11:19; 15:5; 21:22?

### D. Benediction (1 Kings 8:54-61)

What does Solomon attribute to God in these verses?

_____

_____

What is his appeal to the people?

_____

What is meant by being "perfect with the Lord our God"?

_____

### E. Sacrifices (1 Kings 8:62-64)

Notice the large numbers of animals sacrificed. This emphasizes the magnitude of the occasion. What kind of offerings were made?

_____

What did each kind signify?

_____

(Consult the book of Leviticus for help on this question.)

### F. Feast (1 Kings 8:65-66)

The Feast of Tabernacles, lasting seven days, followed the dedication week. Notice here the emphasis on the large number of people participating. The people returned home joyful and glad for what?

_____

Account for the absence of any reference to the Temple building itself as the object of the people's joy.

_____

_____

### G. The Lord's Response (1 Kings 9:1-9)

Read 1 Kings 3:4-5 to refresh your memory concerning God's ear-

49

lier appearance to Solomon. What was God's response to Solomon concerning his present life?

---

What were the conditions laid down for the future?

---

Solomon did not live to see the Temple destroyed and Judah taken captive to Babylon (586 B.C.). But he had already prayed to God that, should ever the people sin and so be taken captive in a foreign land, He would forgive their sin if they confessed it and would bring them back to the land (1 Kings 8:46-53).

## II. COMMENTS

The dedication of the Temple was a never-to-be-forgotten event. How impressive must have been every detail of this sacred ceremony! So vividly is it all pictured that one can almost see the great crowd of elders and chief men of Israel, whom Solomon had summoned to Jerusalem, bringing up the Ark of the Lord into the Temple; the king and elders sacrificing sheep and oxen that could not be numbered for multitude; also the white-robed priests, singers, and musicians pouring forth their praise and thanksgiving as one man to God. And then, as all the people looked toward the Temple and praise ascended from every heart, the Lord Himself descended and took possession of the Temple, manifesting His presence in the cloud and in the glory that filled the house.

This was the climax of Israel's national history, when king and priests, leaders and people, with one accord welcomed to their midst their Maker, Redeemer, and King. Jehovah appeared in His glory to dwell in the house that had been built for Him. (Read the account of a similar scene in Exodus 40:33-35.)

"Israel alone of all nations has provided us with an example of theocratic government in which Jehovah has shown Himself as dwelling among His people. . . . The outward, visible sign afforded Israel of the Divine Presence in their midst was a temple standing high on the hill of Zion," according to H. J. Carpenter.

Facing the Temple, Solomon addressed his opening words to God. Then, turning and facing the people, he blessed them as they stood. Solomon's address consisted simply in recalling God's promises to David and pointing out their fulfillment. His prayer has been well designated "A prayer for all conditions of men." Truly, in every kind of difficulty God's people should turn to Him for help.

Notice how this prayer of Solomon anticipated the time when Gentiles would seek the Lord (1 Kings 8:41-43); also the time of Israel's exile (1 Kings 8:46-47). See how Solomon recognized that real heart repentance was necessary before forgiveness for sin was possible (vv. 47-50). And notice how sin was pointed out as the cause of much of Israel's chastisement (2 Chron. 6:24-25, 36-39).

When Solomon had concluded his prayer, he turned again to the people with words of blessing and exhortation (1 Kings 8:54-61). Then a wonderful thing took place by which God indicated His acceptance of the work that had been accomplished. Fire came down from heaven. This fresh evidence of divine approval called forth from king and people a mighty response in sacrifices (1 Kings 8:62-63; 1 Chron. 7:4-5). This dedicatory sacrifice made by king and people was so huge as to require the use of the whole of the center of the inner court as a mighty altar (1 Kings 8:64; 2 Chron. 7:7).

At the end of fourteen days of feasting, the people returned to their homes, "glad and merry in heart for the goodness that the Lord had shewed unto David, and to Solomon, and to Israel his people" (1 Kings 8:65-66; 2 Chron. 7:8-10).

The second appearance of the Lord to Solomon was probably soon after the completion of the Temple and the royal palace. On this occasion God told Solomon that He had heard his prayer and had answered the part of his petition that concerned the Temple; but that the part of his petition concerning the continuance of the kingdom would be granted only upon the condition of obedience and loyalty to Him.

The fearful consequences of disobedience and disloyalty to God are clearly set forth in 1 Kings 9:6-9 and 2 Chronicles 7:19-22, and they form an exact prophecy of what took place later in the history of the nation.

## III. SUMMARY

Referring back to the survey outline of 1 Kings 8:1–9:9, we may summarize this passage by noting the time elements prominent in the section of the four sections:

| | |
|---|---|
| 8:1-11 | The LEADERS pointed to the *past*, for the Ark and the holy vessels that they moved to the Temple spoke of Israel's past. |
| 8:12-61 | SOLOMON recalled the *past*, and on that basis prayed concerning the *present* and *future*. |

51

8:62-66  The PEOPLE celebrated the occasion of the *present*, as they feasted before the Lord for fourteen days.

9:1-9  The LORD accepted the presentation (*present*) of the Temple to His services and reiterated that continued blessings were contingent upon continued obedience in the *future*.

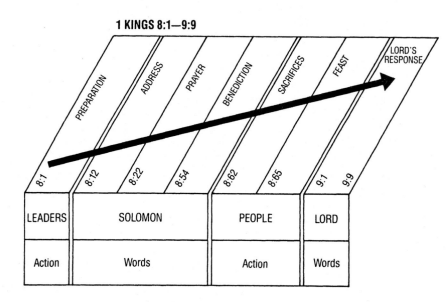

1 KINGS 8:1—9:9

# The Prosperity of the Kingdom and the Apostasy of the King

In this last lesson on Solomon's life, we shall study one of the most important truths of Scripture. Stated negatively, it is: The *true* wealth of a man is not to be measured by the abundance of earthy and transient treasures he may possess. In fame and wisdom, riches and honor, position and popularity, Solomon exceeded all the other kings of the earth. But Solomon, overwhelmed by all of this, forgot the Lord, who really was the One who gave him every good thing he had. The last part of Solomon's life was a tragedy. "Though he began so well, the tragedy of his gradual apostasy had more disastrous results than the infamous scandal of his father, who sincerely repented. . . ."[1]

This lesson is a study of contrasts, centered on these two subjects: the prosperity of the kingdom and the apostasy of the king. Review the survey chart of 1 Kings shown on page 19, recalling all that the book has recorded up to this point. Be in the habit of continually referring to the survey as you proceed from lesson to lesson.

**PART 1:**
**THE PROSPERITY OF THE KINGDOM**
(1 Kings 9:10–10:29; 2 Chron. 8:1–9:28)

## I. ANALYSIS

The Kings and Chronicles passages are similar. Try reading this account first in a modern version, for example the Berkeley, for a clearer understanding of such things as the dollar-equivalent of

1. Merrill C. Tenney, ed., *Zondervan Pictorial Bible Dictionary* (Grand Rapids: Zondervan, 1963), p. 802.

the gold of Solomon's treasury. You will find such a reading helpful.

Following the procedure of this manual, we will concentrate our study in the Kings narrative.

**A. Solomon's Building Programs** (1 Kings 9:10-28; 2 Chron. 8:1-18)

1. *Rebuilding twenty cities in Galilee* (vv. 10-14). (Actually the restoration aspect of this project is recorded only in 2 Chron. 8:1-2. The Kings passage cites only the problem of the unfair bargain Solomon had made with Hiram by offering such unproductive marshland. Read v. 14 thus: "Hiram had paid the king sixscore talents of gold [$3,500,000] for them.") These cities had originally been given by God to Israel for their possession. Did Solomon do right in giving them away to a foreign nation?

_____

_____

2. *Building new cities* (vv. 15-22). Locate the places on a map, noting the geographical extent of Solomon's kingdom.
3. *Officers of the building projects* (v. 23).
4. *Building the Millo* (v. 24). This may have been the fortification covering the breach David had made in the wall of Jebus (cf. 1 Kings 11:27). For "But" in this verse, read "As soon as."
5. *The Ark, the Temple, and the offerings* (v. 25). Read 2 Chronicles 8:12-16 for a fuller description of this. What may be said about Solomon from this?

_____

_____

6. Building a navy (vv. 26-28). Locate Ezion-geber on the map. How important are mercantile ships to an international power?

_____

_____

**B. Visit of the Queen of Sheba** (1 Kings 10:1-13; 2 Chron. 9:1-12)

On the location of this queen's domain *The Wycliffe Bible Commentary* writes, "The queen of Sheba has been identified as the

54

ruler of the Sabeans (Job 1:15), who inhabited Arabia Felix, or the greater part of the territory of the Yemen."[2] (Cf. Gen. 25:3) Study carefully verse 9. How true were the queen's words?

The queen was impressed beyond words with the wisdom and prosperity of Solomon. Recall how both of these entered into Solomon's earlier experience with God by way of a dream (1 Kings 3:5-15).

**C. Solomon's Exceeding Riches** (1 Kings 19:14-29; 2 Chron. 9:13-28)

Read this section with the following money equivalents in mind (these can only be approximate, in view of the variable dollar value):

| | | |
|---|---|---|
| verse 14: | 666 talents of gold— | $20,000,000 |
| 16: | 600 shekels of gold— | $6,000 |
| 17: | 3 pounds of gold— | $1,800 |
| 29: | 600 shekels of silver— | $400 |

Observe especially the paragraph about horses (26-29). Identify Solomon's guilt in light of the Mosaic prohibition of Deuteronomy 17:16.

Before proceeding to the next section, think over the passage you have just studied. Considering all the possible implications of the setting, what were the potential threats to the spiritual health of Solomon and his kingdom? For example, read Deuteronomy 17:16-20, and note the prohibition for a king to "greatly multiply to himself silver and gold." Riches in themselves are not evil, or God would not have given them to Solomon (1 Kings 3:13). What then was the intent of this prohibition, and what was the temptation to Solomon during these prosperous years?

Read Jesus' reference to Solomon's glory in Matthew 6:27-30. Notice how He compares Solomon, the lilies, and the believers in regard to raiment.

2. Charles F. Pfeiffer and Everett F. Harrison, eds., *The Wycliffe Bible Commentary* (Chicago: Moody, 1962), pp. 320-21.

## II. COMMENTS

If ever a man had cause to be grateful to God and an incentive to be true to Him, it was Solomon. Not only had God given him unprecedented earthly honor and material blessings, but He had appeared to him twice, promising him still further favor on the condition of obedience and loyalty.

People from all parts of the earth came to Solomon to hear his wisdom. Among them was the queen of Sheba. Attracted by what she had heard of this great king of Israel, she journeyed all the way to Jerusalem from her distant country to learn for herself whether the reports of his wisdom and wealth had been exaggerated. She was filled with wonder at all she heard and saw, and she was lavish in her praise and in her gifts.

In her address to Solomon, the queen revealed a keen grasp of the relationship between Israel and God. (1) She referred to the throne of Israel as *God's* throne; (2) she declared that it was *God* who put Solomon on the throne; (3) she stated the purpose for which he was placed there: "to be king for the Lord thy God"; (4) she said that Solomon was made king "because thy God loved Israel, to establish them for ever"; and finally, (5) she reminded him that he was placed on the throne "to do judgment and justice."

Before the queen returned to her land, she followed the custom of international protocol by exchanging gifts with the king. Her gift to Solomon was about $3,500,000 plus precious stones and spices.

The last half of this tenth chapter of 1 Kings gives us some idea of Solomon's wealth. A veritable stream of gold poured into Jerusalem continuously. The yearly revenue mentioned in verse 14 would amount to about 20 million dollars, plus such income as is mentioned in verses 15, 22, 25. In addition to all this was the wealth represented by his chariots, horses, navies, and armies.

Verses 16-21 describe something of the splendor and luxury of Jerusalem. The city might well have been called the city of gold. Someone has written, "Gold was the symbol of Solomon's reign, as it was the material by which his palace and its furniture was adorned."

With all this peace, prosperity, and power, the people of Israel must have felt that the golden age had come. Perhaps they were tempted to feel proud and complacent in their possessions and achievements, as though they by their own power had attained them. They greatly needed the warning of Deuteronomy 6:10-15.

## PART 2:
### The Apostasy of the King
(1 Kings 11:1-43)

Chapters 10 and 11 of 1 Kings present two sharply contrasting pictures of Solomon. In chapter 10 we see Solomon as he appeared to others. In chapter 11 we see him as he appeared to God. "The Lord seeth not as man seeth; for man looketh on the outward appearance, but the Lord looketh on the heart" (1 Sam. 16:7). Looking at the *outward appearance* of Solomon, there was everything to be desired by the natural man; but looking at the *heart* of Solomon, there was nothing to be desired by a holy God (vv. 9-11).

Note the ominous word with which chapter 11 begins: "But." The word here implies that the consequence that naturally would be expected did not follow. The consequence that naturally would be expected was that Solomon, having had such abundant grace and blessing bestowed upon him, would delight to do God's will in every particular. But the opposite was true. Gradually he had crowded God out of his life, so that at the time of this chapter his home was a harem and his temple the high places of false gods.

## I. ANALYSIS

This is one of the key chapters of 1 Kings, for it describes the causes that brought about the division of the kingdom (chap. 12). Study it carefully to discover what it says about man and about God.

For an overview of the chapter, read it through first in one sitting. Make a note of main observations and impressions.

Next study the accompanying work sheet, noting how the chapter has been divided into paragraphs. After you have become acquainted with this paragraph-to-paragraph structure, analyze the text of each paragraph. As you study each paragraph, jot down key words and phrases in the rectangular boxes of the work sheet. Let the work sheet be a depository of your observations. This will prove to be a valuable visual aid to your methodical study. It will help to emphasize prominent items, and it will also suggest relations between the various parts of the chapter.

1. Read 11:1-8. List the sins of which Solomon was guilty.

_____

_____

## 1 KINGS 11

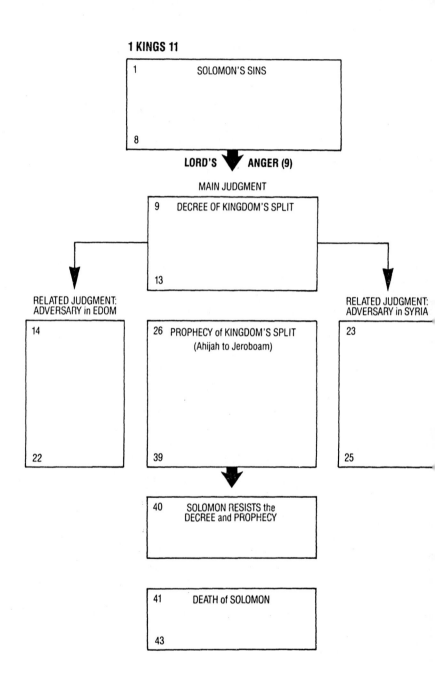

| 1 | SOLOMON'S SINS |
| 8 | |

**LORD'S** ▼ **ANGER (9)**

MAIN JUDGMENT

| 9 | DECREE OF KINGDOM'S SPLIT |
| 13 | |

RELATED JUDGMENT:
ADVERSARY in EDOM

| 14 | |
| 22 | |

| 26 | PROPHECY of KINGDOM'S SPLIT<br>(Ahijah to Jeroboam) |
| 39 | |

RELATED JUDGMENT:
ADVERSARY in SYRIA

| 23 | |
| 25 | |

| 40 | SOLOMON RESISTS the<br>DECREE and PROPHECY |

| 41 | DEATH of SOLOMON |
| 43 | |

Is there any suggestion here that Solomon went gradually deeper and deeper in sin?

How explicit was the Lord's prohibition of verse 2?

What is the impact of the two references to Solomon's father?

Consult a Bible encyclopedia for a description of the gods mentioned: Ashtoreth, Milcom, Chemosh, Molech. How corrupt had Solomon become?

2. Read 11:9-13. Account for the inclusion of the phrase "which had appeared unto him twice."

For what two reasons did God say He would spare some of the kingdom?

What do your learn from this?

3. Read 11:14-22. Locate the kingdom of Edom on the map. Note how God sometimes uses nations to serve the purposes of His divine judgment (14a). Explain 22b ("Nothing: howbeit let me go in any wise") in the light of the sovereign purposes of God.

Read 11:25 to see how Hadad troubled Solomon.
4. Read 11:23-25. Locate Damascus on the map. Notice its strategic position on the trade route to Assyria and Babylon. Rezon was one of those who escaped at the time of David's conquest of Zobah and Syria (read 2 Sam. 8:3-5). What was the extent of Rezon's opposition to Israel?

5. Read 11:26-39. How did Ahijah's prophecy to Jeroboam concur with the Lord's decree made earlier to Solomon?

_____

_____

Was Jeroboam of royal lineage?

_____

What tribes did "Israel" of verse 37 comprise?

_____

Notice that Jeroboam was promised the blessing of God *if* he would fulfill the conditions. Refer to the chart of Kings and Prophets and note that neither Jeroboam nor any king succeeding him fulfilled the conditions.

6. Read 11:40. Ahijah's prophetic disclosure to Jeroboam was made privately. How do you suppose Solomon heard of it (implied by 40*a*)?

_____

Solomon had heard the decree of a rent kingdom *directly from God.* In seeking to kill Jeroboam, whom was Solomon really fighting?

_____

_____

7. Read 11:41-43. Notice how the biography closes in a matter-of-fact way, without any full description of final tragic events in Solomon's life. Only the common formal obituary is recorded (cf. 2 Chron. 9:29-31). What may be learned from this?

_____

_____

8. As a concluding study, think back over this chapter, and list some of the important spiritual lessons it teaches in areas such as: man, God, sin, responsibility, opportunity, obedience, judgment, sovereignty of God, world history.

_____

_____

_____

_____

_____

## II. COMMENTS

1. Long before the Israelites had reached the land of Canaan, God through Moses gave laws that applied to all His people in the land. One of these laws was that they should not marry those of other nations, as such marriages would result in turning the Israelites away from God to idols (Deut. 7:1-4).

2. Also God had anticipated the time when Israel would become dissatisfied with the form of government that He had established for them and would ask for human kings to rule over them so that they might be like other nations (Deut. 17:14-15; cf. 1 Sam. 8:4-5). Solomon certainly was guilty of bringing the foreign pagan element into his own kingdom, making it like all the others.

3. Deuteronomy 17:16-20 records four things Israel's kings were commanded not to do and one thing they were commanded to do. Solomon flagrantly disobeyed each of the four things *forbidden*:

a. "He shall not multiply horses to himself" (1 Kings 10:26)

b. "Nor cause the people to return to Egypt, to the end that he should multiply horses" (1 Kings 10:28-29)

c. "Neither shall he multiply wives to himself, that his heart turn not away" (1 Kings 11:3)

d. "Neither shall he greatly multiply to himself silver and gold" (1 Kings 10:14, 23, 27)

4. The breaking of the four laws mentioned above were sins of *commission*, but Solomon also was guilty of sins of *omission*. Deuteronomy 17:18-20 tells what God commanded to be done by the king. This Solomon failed to do. He probably did not read the Scriptures regularly; he certainly did not obey them. The cause of the ruin that so rapidly followed the splendor of Solomon's reign was *neglect of the Word of God*. All the sin, error, heresy, and worldliness that has ever been in the church has also come from neglect of God's Word—neglect to know it or neglect to obey it.

5. In what sense could Solomon be called wise, when he disobeyed the One who called him and anointed him to be king? James M. Gray writes, "The answer is that the wisdom that he had was of the earthly rather than the heavenly kind. It was sufficient to keep the city, but not to keep his heart. It helped him rule the kingdom, but not his own spirit."

6. The harem of Solomon and the idolatry it fostered indicate the depth of corruptness to which Solomon stooped. H. J. Carpenter says, "It is a pitiable picture of a great king who is drawn away from the piety of his early days, and becomes the puppet of his harem. . . . The steps in the spiritual deterioration and apostasy are

61

indicated with inspired skill. First, he 'went after' the false gods, and 'went not fully after the Lord.' Then he built shrines for them, and allowed his wives to burn incense and sacrifice to their gods. Finally, his heart was 'turned from the Lord his God,' and he who *built* Jehovah's Temple became the foremost of those kings of Israel and Judah who *desecrated* the Temple of God, and turned away the heart of their subjects from the pure worship of the Lord, who had given them the good land of their heritage."

7. Solomon's guilt was great and his punishment heavy, though tempered with mercy for David's sake (1 Kings 11:11-13). The ultimate significance of this is that in the line of David that "greater than Solomon" (Jesus) was to come.

8. We wish it might have been recorded of Solomon, as of David, that when his sin was brought before him and chastisement announced, that he fell before the Lord in true repentance, confessing his guilt and imploring God's forgiveness. The three adversaries of 11:14-40, which constituted thorns in the sides of the erring king, may have been used of God not only for punitive purposes but also to urge him to return to the Lord. As far as we have any record though, no word of repentance fell from Solomon's lips.

9. Although war clouds were arising on Israel's horizon from both the north (Syria) and the south (Edom), the more formidable threat came from within the kingdom in the person of Jeroboam, a young man of Ephraim. This was not a case of rebellion by a disloyal subject but of claim by a divinely appointed ruler.

10. The "*ten* tribes" of 11:31 and the "*one* tribe" of 11:32 do not imply a *lost* tribe of the *twelve*. The "he" of verse 32 refers to Solomon's successors (Rehoboam, etc.), whereas the "one tribe" is that of Benjamin, which remained with Judah. (Cf. 1 Kings 12:21.)

11. Solomon's attitude toward Jeroboam, when he learned that God had chosen him to be king over ten of the twelve tribes of Israel, reminds us of the attitude of King Saul when he learned the Lord's will concerning David. Not a word of repentance. No tears like those of his father. No confession such as came from David. Only one thing is mentioned, only one act is recorded of apostate Solomon—he sought to kill Jeroboam.

12. In some ways Solomon was a type of Christ. Graham Scroggie observes that it is only in a limited way that an Old Testament character can typify Christ. "Moses, and Aaron, and Samson, and David, and others, give a momentary flash of Messianic anticipation, and that is all. It is so also in the case of Solomon. He anticipates Christ as the Temple Builder, and as the King of Peace, but in his personal character he is low even by the standards of his fel-

lows. He rose high and he fell deep. He who prayed the wonderful prayer of 1 Kings 8, kept a vast harem; and he who chose the blessing of wisdom, fell into the completest folly."[3]

## III. SUMMARY OF SOLOMON'S LIFE

1. When Solomon was born, "the Lord loved him" (2 Sam. 12:24). Hence one of the names given him was Jedidiah, meaning "beloved of the Lord."

2. Solomon was anointed successor to King David toward the end of David's life, in the face of a conspiracy to make Adonijah king.

3. Solomon's first of a series of marriages was to the daughter of the king of Egypt. His many idolatrous wives eventually brought about his downfall.

4. Early in Solomon's reign he worshiped and served the Lord with a true heart. The Lord was pleased with his request made when the Lord appeared to him the first time at Gibeon.

5. Solomon was an efficient administrator and energetic leader. Under his reign the boundaries of Israel extended far, from the border of Egypt to the northern Euphrates valley.

6. Solomon was also wise and wealthy. He had a wide knowledge of the sciences and wrote books, proverbs, and songs. As to wealth, his kingdom was made of *gold.*

7. Solomon's biggest project was the Temple and its associated buildings. David had wanted to build the Temple, but Solomon was given this privilege by God.

8. Solomon's reign was generally one of peace, without any major battles or rebellions. Nevertheless, its latter years were declining years, as the king walked farther and farther away from God. He worshiped other gods, sought to kill the man (Jeroboam) who was destined to receive the Northern Kingdom, and died leaving his kingdom on the brink of disaster.

3. *Know Your Bible* (Westwood, N.J.: Revell, n.d.), 1: 71.

# Lesson 7

1 Kings 12:1-33
2 Chronicles 10:1–11:4

# The Kingdom Is Divided

**C**hapter 12 of 1 Kings is a key chapter in the Old Testament because it records the event that steered the course of God's people through the remainder of the Old Testament days.

For a little more than a hundred years (1043-931 B.C.) Israel remained intact as one unified kingdom. Saul, David, and Solomon were its kings, in that order. Solomon began his reign well, but before long he was setting a bad example in living and actually drawing his people away from true worship of God. It was during his reign that the stage was being set for a rupture of the kingdom. As studied in the last lesson, it was at the end of his life that God pronounced that He would rend most of the kingdom out of the hand of the son who would succeed him. The story of the breakup of the kingdom is the subject of this lesson. The diagrammed setting is as follows:

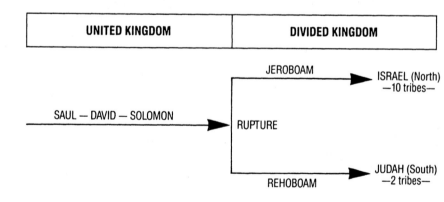

| UNITED KINGDOM | DIVIDED KINGDOM |
|---|---|

SAUL — DAVID — SOLOMON

RUPTURE

JEROBOAM → ISRAEL (North) —10 tribes—

REHOBOAM → JUDAH (South) —2 tribes—

**1 KINGS 12**

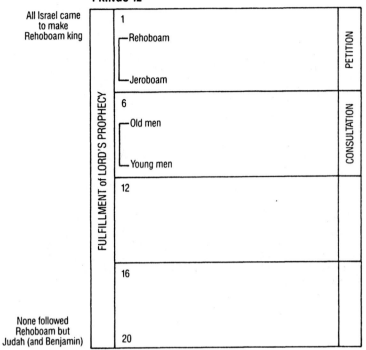

All Israel came
to make
Rehoboam king

FULFILLMENT of LORD'S PROPHECY

| 1 |
| Rehoboam |
| Jeroboam |

PETITION

| 6 |
| Old men |
| Young men |

CONSULTATION

| 12 |

| 16 |

None followed
Rehoboam but
Judah (and Benjamin)

| 20 |

## THE DIVIDED KINGDOM

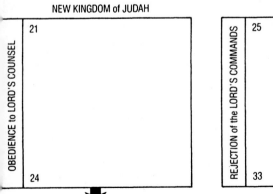

NEW KINGDOM of JUDAH

OBEDIENCE to LORD'S COUNSEL

21

24

NEW KINGDOM of ISRAEL

REJECTION of the LORD'S COMMANDS

25

33

65

## I. ANALYSIS

First mark the paragraph divisions of 1 Kings 12 in your Bible as they appear on the accompanying work sheet. Then read through the chapter, underlining the key words and phrases in your Bible and making a note of your major impressions. Record paragraph titles on the work sheet, in the upper right-hand corner of each paragraph box. What is the main point of each paragraph? Compare your answer with the study shown, beginning "Petition," "Consultation," etc. Record key words and phrases in each paragraph box. After you have studied the accompanying work sheet chart, complete the following exercises.

1. This chapter makes an interesting study in contrasts, with at least one set of contrasts appearing in each paragraph. Complete the study begun on the work sheet (Rehoboam—Jeroboam; old men—young men; etc.).

2. Compare the two paragraphs below the line designated "THE DIVIDED KINGDOM," as to what is taught about the new kingdom of Judah and the new kingdom of Israel.

3. See 12:1-5. Compare the "all" of verse 1 with the "all" of verse 3. How do you explain the change of action?

_____

What was the original cause of Solomon's heavy tax program? (Read 1 Sam. 8:10-17.)

_____

4. See 12:6-11. Account for Rehoboam's rejecting the old men's counsel in favor of that of the young men (v.8). What are the dangers of such a policy?

_____

5. See 12:12-15. Explain: "The king hearkened not unto the people; for the cause was from the Lord" (12:15).

_____

Compare 12:25.

_____

66

6. See 12:16-20. Compare verse 16 with 2 Samuel 20:1. Interpret "the tribe of Judah only" (20b) in the light of verse 21, "with the tribe of Benjamin."

_____

_____

7. See 12:21-24. What key Christian trait is illustrated here?

_____

_____

8. See 12:25-33. Locate these places on a map: Shechem, Penuel, Bethel, Dan. What basically motivated Jeroboam's acts?

_____

_____

Identify the various things he did here in order to accomplish his purpose.

_____

_____

9. Think back over the chapter; then enumerate various spiritual lessons taught here.

_____

_____

What different kinds of sins are exposed in this chapter?

_____

_____

## II. COMMENTS

It should be noted that before the events of this chapter took place there were occasions of hostility between the northern tribes ("men of Israel") and the southern tribes ("men of Judah"). (Read 2 Sam. 19:40-43.) According to the _Cambridge Bible_, "It seems not improbable that the arrangement for this gathering at Shechem was a sort of protest by the men of the north against the southern tribes who, because Jerusalem with the Temple and the royal dwellings were in their part of the land, may have claimed to be the ruling part of the nation."

Although apparently ready to accept Rehoboam as their king, the men of Israel wanted one point settled before they pledged their allegiance. So with their popular leader, Jeroboam, whom they had brought back from Egypt, they came to Rehoboam and stated the condition on which they would acknowledge him king. They wanted the taxes and levies, which had been instituted by Solomon, to be lightened. They had quickly forgotten that these were part of divine judgment for demanding human kings to rule over them (1 Sam. 8:10-17). People and nations should learn from history the universal timeless principle of cause and effect.

Rehoboam's deliberations and consultations resulted in his returning an insulting answer to the men of Israel, whereupon there was an immediate revolt of the ten northern tribes. Rehoboam made one attempt, although an untactful and unsuccessful one, to prevent the breach. He sent Adoram, the chief tax collector, as his messenger to the men of Israel. Adoram was probably the most unwelcome man to appear at that time. To show how they felt about submitting to Rehoboam or about considering any compromise that he might have to propose, the men of Israel stoned Adoram to death. Rehoboam, thoroughly alarmed, fled to Jerusalem; and Jeroboam was made king of the ten tribes.

Safe once more in Jerusalem, Rehoboam planned to quell the rebellion of the ten tribes by force and gathered an army of 180,000 men from the tribes of Judah and Benjamin in preparation. But God interposed by sending a message through the prophet Shemaiah, and the army was dispersed.

Thus the division of the kingdom was an accomplished fact. Jeroboam was now king of the ten tribes, while Rehoboam reigned in Jerusalem over the tribes of Judah and Benjamin and also over such individuals from the ten tribes as dwelt in the cities of Judah (1 Kings 12:17). These were probably men in the service of the royal house. Later on, when Jeroboam had introduced calf worship into the northern kingdom, the Levites and also those from the ten tribes who were true to Jehovah came to dwell in Judah (2 Chron. 11:13-17). Look at the map on page 7, and fix in mind the fact that from this time on the ten tribes, living in the northern part of the land, are spoken of as "Israel," whereas the two tribes (Judah and Benjamin) in the southern part of the land are spoken of as "Judah." Sometimes Israel is also called "the northern kingdom" or "the ten-tribe kingdom." Judah is sometimes called "the southern kingdom."

Now the nation of God was a "kingdom divided against itself." For the remainder of this study of 1 Kings we shall have in view both kingdoms, Israel and Judah, and we shall be alternately looking at the actions of first the one and then the other, as indicated in the outline of pages 20-21. It will be important also to keep constantly before us the chart on page 101. Look at the chart, and note that nineteen different kings reigned over Israel (the ten tribes.) All nineteen were evil men. Not one of them served the Lord. It was different in the kingdom of Judah, for some of Judah's kings were good men.

## ISRAEL'S FIRST KING—JEROBOAM

Jeroboam was the first, and in some respects the worst, of the kings of Israel. He was of humble origin. All we know of his parentage is given in 1 Kings 11:26. He was an efficient and industrious man, as we have already learned (1 Kings 11:28), and probably his promotion by Solomon and his popularity with the discontented people of the northern tribes had turned his head and given him aspirations for power. After his interview with the prophet Ahijah and his recall from Egypt by the men of Israel, the way was clear for the realization of his ambition. He found himself made king over ten of the twelve tribes of God's people.

However, Jeroboam did not acknowledge that it was really God who had given him the throne. God had said, "I will take thee, and thou shalt reign according to all that thy soul desireth" (1 Kings 11:37). Apparently Jeroboam had no intention either of complying with the condition that God had stated for the continuance of his line (1 Kings 11:38). This was the same condition that God had made for the family of David, that is, *obedience*.

If Jeroboam had complied with God's condition of obedience, he could have had God's presence and God's power in building his kingdom. (See the promise that God gave in 1 Kings 11:38.) But Jeroboam ignored God and God's spokesman Ahijah, and God's written Word. The first thing he did after fortifying Shechem to be the royal city was to devise measures from his own heart to establish himself in his kingdom. Read 1 Kings 12:25-28, and notice that it was for political reasons that Jeroboam caused Israel to worship two golden calves at Shechem. "He had no intention of throwing off the yoke Jehovah altogether, but was foolish enough to think He could be worshiped in one way as well as another," according to James M. Gray.

Regardless of the fact that God had appointed the *place* where His people should assemble for worship, had specified those whom He would have act as *priests*, and had set the *time* of the yearly feasts, Jeroboam changed all these. Although God had chosen Jerusalem for religious gatherings, he made Bethel and Dan places of worship. He made priests of the common people, although God had chosen the tribe of Levi to minister in holy things. He pointed the people to the golden calves instead of to the Temple where God dwelt. He told the people it was "too much" for them to go up to Jerusalem, whereas God had commanded all Israel to assemble there for the annual feasts. And Jeroboam changed the date of the Feast of Tabernacles to the eighth month, whereas God had appointed the seventh. (Read 1 Kings 12:2; 8-33.) Notice the expression in 1 Kings 12:33 "the month which he had devised in his own heart." God's Word was completely set aside, and Jeroboam followed the devices of his own heart. This is dangerous to do at any time, since the human heart is "deceitful above all things, and desperately wicked." God's Word is the only absolute guide for human conduct.

## III. SUMMARY

A prominent place in the action of 1 Kings 12 is that of the word of the Lord. Viewed from this angle, the chapter may be divided into three parts, summarized thus:

1. Fulfillment of the Lord's prophecy      (12:1-20)
   —the kingdom splits
2. Obedience to the Lord's counsel        (12:21-24)
   —Rehoboam refrains from war
3. Rejection of the Lord's commands      (12:25-33)
   —Jeroboam fosters idolatry

# Lesson 8

# Antagonisms Between Israel and Judah

The kingdoms of Israel and Judah survived as two separate peoples for about two hundred years (931-722 B.C.). The relationships between the kingdoms are marked by the following three periods:

|  | about 60 years | about 75 years | about 75 years |
|---|---|---|---|
|  | ANTAGONISMS (Israel vs. Judah) | ALLIANCES (Israel and Judah) | ANTAGONISMS (Israel vs. Judah) |
| ISRAEL | 931<br>Jeroboam to Omri | 874<br>Ahab to Jehoahaz | 798        722<br>Jehoash to Hoshea |
| JUDAH | 931<br>Rehoboam to Asa | 873<br>Jehoshaphat to Joash | 796<br>Amaziah to Ahaz |

In this lesson we shall study about the reigns of the kings of Israel and Judah during the first period. As noted in Lesson 1, the writer of Kings alternates back and forth between Israel and Judah in reporting the reigns of the kings. The kings of these chapters of 1 Kings appear in this order:

| ISRAEL | JUDAH | ISRAEL |
|---|---|---|
| 1. Jeroboam | 2. Rehoboam<br>3. Abijam<br>4. Asa | 5. Nadab<br>6. Baasha<br>7. Elah<br>8. Zimri<br>9. Omri |

Keep in mind as you study this lesson that learning the facts of Bible history (important as the facts themselves are) is not the

**1 KINGS 13:1—16:28**

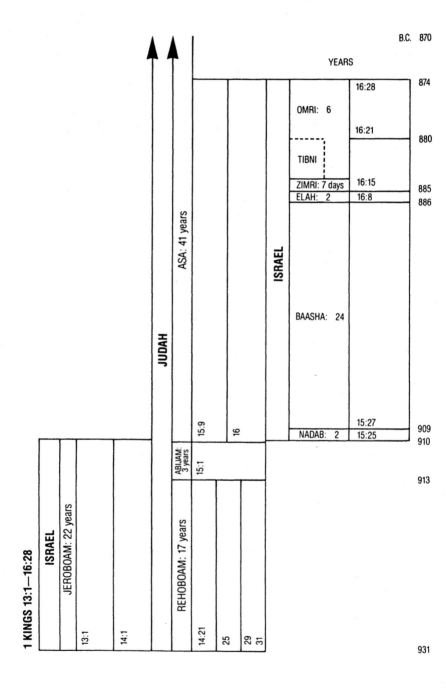

ultimate goal of your study. Such facts illustrate and teach certain timeless universal truths. When you derive these truths from your study, you are ready to apply ancient Bible history to this present day.

## I. ANALYSIS

The accompanying work sheet will help you organize all the facts of this historical narrative. You may choose to transfer the work sheet outline to a large piece of paper in order to give you more space for recording.

As you read the text of 1 Kings, record key words, phrases, and events in the appropriate boxes or in the margins. Let these recorded observations be starting points for further observations, including comparisons, contrasts, etc. When you have finished this, proceed with the following study suggestions:

1. How is 13:1 related to 12:33?

_____

_____

_____

Notice how explicit is the prophecy of 12:2. Read 2 Kings 23:15-20 to see how accurately the prophecy was fulfilled. Note how small was Jeroboam's request for prayer (13:6) in comparison with his need.

What important lesson is taught by the judgment that fell on the "man of God out of Judah"? (13:11-25)

_____

How do you account for the old prophet's feelings, recorded in 13:26-32?

_____

_____

Does 13:33a suggest that a door was opened for Jeroboam to repent of his evil way?

_____

_____

Notice that anyone ("whosoever would") could be a priest in Jeroboam's administration.

2. See 14:1-20. Why did Jeroboam not want to see the prophet himself?

_____

Why did he have his wife disguised?

_____

Analyze 14:7-11 for God's appraisal of Jeroboam's reign and the judgment decreed. Note also the prophecy of captivity in 14:15-16, which was fulfilled in 722 B.C., when the ten tribes were taken captive to Assyria. What does 14:13b reveal concerning the heart of Jeroboam's son?

_____

Note what is said in 2 Chronicles 13:19-20 regarding the death of Jeroboam.
3. See 14:21-31 (Rehoboam). Read chapters 11 and 12 of 2 Chronicles for a more complete description of the reign of Rehoboam. Then answer the following questions. Observe from the chart on page 102 that during most of the time Jeroboam reigned over Israel, Rehoboam reigned over Judah. Why did Rehoboam fortify cities of Judah? (2 Chron. 11:5-12; 1 Kings 14:30)

_____

Were all of the seventeen years of Rehoboam's rule evil? (Compare 2 Chron. 11:14, 16-17; 12:1, with 1 Kings 14:22-24.)

_____

Note how Jerusalem is described in 1 Kings 14:21; then relate this to what happened to Jerusalem according to 1 Kings 14:25-28.

_____

What does 2 Chronicles 12:2-12 disclose as to the causes of this attack?

_____

Why did Rehoboam do evil (2 Chron. 12:14; compare 2 Chron. 27:6 and 1 Chron. 29:18)?

_____

_____

74

Three times it is stated the Rehoboam's mother was an Ammonitess (1 Kings 14:21, 31; 2 Chron. 12:13). What is the significance of this? (cf. 1 Kings 11:1-2)

4. See 15:1-8 (Abijam). Read 2 Chronicles 13 for a longer description of Abijam. What can you say about his faith on the basis of his testimony of 2 Chronicles 13:4-12?

How do you reconcile this with 1 Kings 15:3?

5. See 15:9-24 (Asa). How many years did Asa reign?

Note from the accompanying work sheet that the throne of Israel changed rulers often during the rule of Judah's King Asa. Read 2 Chronicles 14-16 for its full description of Asa's reign. Identify these four major eras or events of his career as recorded in 2 Chronicles:
    (a) 2 Chronicles 14:1-8
    (b) 14:9-15
    (c) Chapter 15
    (d) Chapter 16
6. See 15:25–16:28 (Nadab to Omri). Observe the repeated cycle of sin and judgment. Were there any reforms or revivals in Israel at this time?

Did God speak to Israel through any prophet during these years?

What does revelation have to do with accountability?

In your own words, characterize the reigns of each of these kings:
Nadab:

Baasha:

Elah:

Zimri:

_____

Omri:

_____

7. List some major spiritual lessons taught by these chapters of Kings and Chronicles. Apply them to nations and individuals today.

_____

_____

_____

_____

How does the prominence of divine judgment in the Old Testament throw light on the doctrine of atonement by Christ's blood?

_____

_____

_____

## II. COMMENTS

### A. Jeroboam

Even in Jeroboam's wickedness (last lesson) God sought to bring this willful king to repentance. At Bethel, while Jeroboam was sacrificing and burning incense to one of the golden calves that he had made, God's messenger appeared, delivered a message, and performed a miracle that ought to have convinced Jeroboam of the authority and displeasure of God. As if that were not enough warning to Jeroboam, God showed him that even God's prophets are judged for the sin of disobedience to the word of God. King Jeroboam ought to have seen a picture of himself, and his own fate if he did not repent, by the fate of the prophet from Judah. Jeroboam, like the prophet, had been chosen by God for a high position. Also like the prophet, he knew perfectly well what God would have him do. But like the prophet, he had disobeyed the word of God.

One would think that this dramatic occurrence, coming so soon after the miracles of the riven altar and the paralyzed hand, would have convinced Jeroboam of God's power and His sure punishment for disobedience. But note what is written of him in 1 Kings 13:33-34. Jeroboam's heart was set on sin. He led his people into such idolatry and wickedness and defiance of God that ever after in the history of the nation he is referred to as "Jeroboam the son of Nebat, who made Israel to sin."

We read of the final judgment of Jeroboam in chapter 14 of 1 Kings. When death threatened his beloved son, the king turned to the prophet of God. Apparently he was ashamed to face the prophet after his continued and obstinate career of sinfulness, for he sent his wife the queen, disguised so that she would not be recognized. But although the prophet Ahijah was blind, God revealed to him who his visitor was; and God gave him a message for Jeroboam that was indeed 'heavy tidings.'"

All the fearful judgments spoken through Ahijah came to pass. Besides the judgments on Jeroboam's own house, the whole kingdom suffered. As we proceed in the study of this book we shall see how Israel was smitten "as a reed is shaken in the water." Israel was rooted out of her land and scattered beyond the river; Israel was indeed given up by God. All this because of Jeroboam "who did sin, and who made Israel to sin."

### B. Rehoboam

Rehoboam reigned over Judah for one year as co-regent with his father, Solomon, and for sixteen years alone. It appears that during the first three years of his reign both he and the people served the Lord. Then things took a downward turn. Judah provoked God to jealousy by their sins, and God, using Egypt as a rod with which to chastise Judah for their disobedience, allowed the Egyptians to come up in the fifth year of Rehoboam's reign and seize the treasures of the Temple and the royal palace in Jerusalem. This was a great loss to Judah.

Note however that Rehoboam was not altogether hardened, as Jeroboam appears to have been. Rehoboam and his people humbled themselves under God's chastening and rebuke, and God's further judgments were stayed. Rehoboam was buried in the city of David, and his son Abijam reigned in his stead.

### C. Abijam

Abijam was the son of Rehoboam and his favorite wife, Maachah. Maachah was probably the granddaughter of Absalom. (Note: The Hebrew word translated "daughter" indicates lineage but not necessarily of the first generation. The word may mean "granddaughter," "great-granddaughter," etc. The same applies to the word "son.") Absalom had one daughter called Tamar (2 Sam. 14:27), wife of Uriel, whose daughter was Maachah (or Michaiah, 2 Chron. 13:2).

According to 1 Kings 15:3, Abijam's reign was evil, for he walked "in all the sins of his father." But in 2 Chronicles 13 we see him testifying to trust in God: "But as for us, the Lord is our God, and we have not forsaken him" (2 Chron. 13:10). There are two possible explanations of this apparent contradiction:

1. 2 Chronicles 13 records principally Abijam's *words*. What he *said* was good, but what he *did* was another thing, in spite of his pious talk. If this explanation is correct, we have in 2 Chronicles 13 a classic example of hypocrisy.

2. The other view is that Abijam began his three-year reign well, and that his victory against Jeroboam was for his faith in God. But soon he forgot the Lord and began to trust himself, taking on the ways of other evil kings, such as marrying many wives. This short phrase of 2 Chronicles 13:21 indicates such a turn in his life: "But Abijah waxed mighty, and married fourteen wives." First Kings 15:3 evaluates his evil reign as a whole.

Two passages stand out in this record of Abijam:

1. 2 Chronicles 13:4-12. Here is given a treatise on the implications of covenant relationship with God ("covenant of salt," v. 5, is so described because the preservation quality of salt symbolizes the covenant's permanent, immutable character; cf. Num. 18:19 and Lev. 2:13).

2. 1 Kings 15:4-5. Here is shown the mercy and grace of God in perpetuating the dynasty of Judah only for David's sake.

### D. Asa

The life of Asa differed greatly from the lives of the two kings who had immediately preceded him on the throne of Judah. Asa began reigning while Israel's first king, Jeroboam, was yet on the throne (1 Kings 15:9), and Ahab, Israel's seventh king, had ascended the throne before Asa's reign over Judah came to a close (1 Kings 16:29). (See chart on page 102.) Whereas all these seven kings of Israel were evil, Asa was a man whose heart was "perfect" before God. This of course does not mean that Asa was faultless. He did things for which he was rebuked, things that showed weak faith in God. He made mistakes, got angry, and sinned; nevertheless, like David he was willing to do God's will. He aimed to do God's will rather than his own, although he sometimes fell under temptation. (The Hebrew word for "perfect" in such verses as 1 Kings 15:14 is *shālēm*, meaning "whole." The word suggests wholeheartedness in loyalty.)

Some of the highlights of Asa's career are as follows:

1. Asa was young when he came to the throne, but he immediately began much needed reforms in Judah. He even removed his grandmother from the influential position of queen grandmother because of her idolatry.

2. For the first ten years of Asa's reign there was no war. During this time of peace he took opportunity to fortify many cities of Judah, not forgetting to point out to his people that God had given them rest on every side.

3. Then came a war with the Ethiopians that tested Asa's faith in God. A great army invaded Judah from the south, so great that Asa had no hope of gaining the victory in his own strength. It was not in his own strength that he went into this war. His prayer showed how implicit was his faith in God, and God honored his faith.

4. But God knows the human heart. He knows how prone men are, after a great victory, to trust in their own strength and wisdom and to fail in their dependence upon God. So He sent a message of warning to King Asa and the victorious army as they were returning from the war (2 Chron. 15:1-7). The prophet's words stirred Asa to still greater zeal; and as he led the people in sacrifice and praise to God, the religious fervor reached a high pitch (2 Chron. 15:8-15).

5. In the thirty-sixth year of Asa's reign, Baasha, king of Israel, became aggressive, threatening the security of Judah. He made the daring attempt to use the city of Ramah, which was situated not far from Jerusalem, as a fortress. Baasha's success in the enterprise as outlined would have meant the complete isolation and domination of Jerusalem, Judah's capital (2 Chron. 16:1; 1 Kings 15:17). Baasha's project had to be stopped, but how? Asa had apparently forgotten the means by which victory was won in his war with the Ethiopians. Instead of praying, he made a league with the heathen king Ben-hadad of Syria (1 Kings 15:18-19; 2 Chron. 16:2-3). It is a sad thing to see King Asa, whose trust in God had once been so remarkable, display such fear and lack of faith.

6. Although Asa's league with Ben-hadad brought a military victory, it also brought a stern rebuke from the Lord and a sentence of continued war as punishment for trusting in the arm of flesh rather than in Jehovah. (Read 2 Chron. 16:7-9; Jer. 17:5.) If Asa had trusted in God he could have put to flight the whole Syrian army, to say nothing of Israel's army.

7. In the later years of his life Asa backslid from the high plane on which he started his reign. Instead of repenting when the prophet brought God's message to him, he went into a rage and imprisoned the messenger, Hanani. And when God sent him

chastisement in the form of diseased feet, "he sought not to the Lord, but to the physicians" (2 Chron. 16:12-14).

### E. Nadab

Nadab began his reign over Israel in the second year of Asa's reign over Judah. He reigned only two years. All that is said of him, except the manner of his death, is that he did evil in the sight of the Lord (perhaps not in the eyes of his subjects), "and walked in the way of his father, and in his sin wherewith he made Israel to sin" (1 Kings 15:25-26).

### F. Baasha

Baasha was from the tribe of Issachar. He gained the throne of Israel by conspiring against and slaying King Nadab, while he was engaged in a war with the Philistines at Gibbethon (1 Kings 15:27-28). Baasha then proceeded to exterminate the whole house of Jeroboam. This was in fulfillment of the prediction of 1 Kings 14:10-11.

Throughout the twenty-four years of Baasha's reign there were hostilities between him and the king of Judah, but he was unsuccessful in his attempt to invade Judah, as we have already learned in our study of Asa's reign.

Although Baasha executed the sentence that God had pronounced against the house of Jeroboam, he did not learn a lesson from it. Judgment had fallen on Jeroboam's house because Jeroboam had sinned. But instead of taking this as a warning to himself, Baasha continued to sin in the same way that Jeroboam had done. So God pronounced the same judgment upon Baasha.

### G. Elah

Elah succeeded his father, Baasha, on the throne of Israel, but reigned only a very short time. A drunken, worthless fellow, he was murdered by Zimri, one of his captains, as he was in the midst of a drunken debauch at Tirzah, while his army was still at Gibbethon warring with the Philistines.

### H. Zimri

Zimri did to the house of Baasha what Baasha had done to the house of Jeroboam (1 Kings 16:11-13).

Zimri, who held the throne of Israel only seven days, was evidently unpopular with the army. As soon as the news that Zimri had murdered King Elah and claimed the throne for himself reached the army at Gibbethon, the soldiers made Omri, captain of the host, king over Israel. Then they went with him to Tirzah, the royal city, and besieged it. When Zimri saw that the city was taken and that there was no hope of his retaining the throne, he entered the palace and committed suicide.

## Omri

Omri was the sixth king to occupy the throne of the ten-tribe kingdom. After subduing the rival claimant to the throne, he reigned over Israel twelve years. For the first six years he reigned in Tirzah. He then selected for the new capital a hill that is most admirably located for beauty and defense. He purchased the hill from Shemer and named it, and the city that he built, Samaria, after the former owner. The city continued to be the capital and center of Israel's political life throughout the existence of the ten-tribe kingdom. Archaeological discoveries reveal that Omri was a famous king throughout the world of his day.

## III. SUMMARY

For the first sixty-year period of the divided kingdom there was constant war and antagonism between the two kingdoms. Of the two, the southern tribes (Judah and Benjamin) had the brighter history, enjoying many years of spiritual blessing with military victory and material prosperity. The northern ten tribes were continually plagued by the corruptions of idolatry and vice, which brought rebellion, bloodshed, conspiracy, and unrest for the whole extent of the period. In the south, one dynasty remained intact. In the north, dynasty gave way to dynasty.

Over and over God demonstrated to Israel and Judah in various ways that His eyes "run to and fro throughout the whole earth," showing Himself strong in behalf of those whose heart is "full of integrity toward Him" (Berkeley) and bringing judgment to those who persist in unrighteousness (2 Chron. 16:9).

# Lesson 9

# The Prophet Elijah

Elijah, the prophet of God, and Ahab, the wicked king of Israel, are the two most conspicuous figures throughout the last six chapters of 1 Kings. In our present lesson we shall be almost wholly occupied with the prophet Elijah. Read Matthew 17:3, and note how Elijah is paired with Moses. As Moses was the key representative of the Law, Elijah was the key representative of the Prophets.

In Lesson 8 we studied one of the darkest periods in Israel's history. But Israel was brought into still thicker darkness under Ahab. As if his following in the sins of Jeroboam seemed trifling, he further provoked the Lord God of Israel to anger by his marriage with the heathen princess Jezebel, an ardent Baal worshiper who was zealously determined to stamp out the worship of Jehovah in Israel and substitute Baal worship. Once this false religion was introduced, it flourished to such an extent that soon the worship of God seemed utterly forgotten. Of all the hundreds of thousands in Israel, only seven thousand remained true to God. F. B. Meyer remarks that even "these seven thousand were so paralyzed by fear and kept so still that their very existence was unknown to Elijah in the hour of his greatest loneliness."

From one vantage point the Bible narrative studied in this lesson is bright in contrast to that of the last lesson, which was mainly about the activities of sinful kings who lived their lives with no recognition of God's presence or authority. In this lesson the spotlight is on Elijah, a true servant of God living in constant recognition of God's presence and authority. All these wicked kings may have enjoyed a short season of prominence and earthly success, but they passed on into oblivion. Their names are scarcely mentioned or remembered in all subsequent history. But Elijah, who walked and talked with God throughout his earthly career, was taken to heaven in a chariot of fire, stood with Christ on the mount of transfiguration, and throughout the eternal ages will live continually in the presence of our Lord and Saviour Jesus Christ. It pays to serve God.

In Old Testament times God spoke to the fathers in various ways by men called prophets (Heb. 1:1). God did not *always* speak by prophets, but He *often* did so. Study the chart of page 102, and notice again the two groups of prophets: (1) during the latter half of the kingdoms the prophets were those who wrote books of our Bible; (2) during the first part of the kingdoms the prophets were not authors of any complete prophetic book in the Bible. The following list compiled by J. Barton Payne identifies those earlier prophets and their ministries.[1]

| NAME | MINISTRY | REFERENCE |
|------|----------|-----------|
| Ahijah | appointed and deposed Jeroboam | 1 Kings 11:29, 14:2 |
| Shemaiah | stopped Rehoboam's war; | 1 Kings 12:22; |
| | humbled him | 2 Chronicles 12:5 |
| Anonymous | condemned Jeroboam for his sin | 1 Kings 13:1 |
| Azariah | aroused Asa to reform | 2 Chronicles 15:1 |
| Jehu (son of Hanani) | condemned Baasha's sin | 1 Kings 16:1 |
| Hanani | condemned Asa's Aramean mercenaries | 2 Chronicles 16:7 |
| Elijah | condemned Ahab (no rain) | 1 Kings 17:1 |
| | challenged Ahab | 1 Kings 18:17 |
| Anonymous | promised Ahab two victories | 1 Kings 20:13, 22, 28 |
| | condemned his leniency | 1 Kings 20:38 |
| Elijah | condemned Ahab's murder of Naboth | 1 Kings 21:17 |
| Micaiah | condemned Ahab's Ramoth campaign | 1 Kings 22:8 |
| Jehu (son of Hanani) | condemned Jehoshaphat's alliance with north | 2 Chronicles 19:2 |
| Jahaziel | promised Jehoshaphat victory | 2 Chronicles 20:14 |
| Eliezer | condemned Jehoshaphat's ship alliance | 2 Chronicles 20:37 |
| Elijah | condemned Ahaziah of Israel | 2 Kings 1:3 |
| Elisha | advised Jehoshaphat against Moab | 2 Kings 3:13 |
| Elijah | condemned Jehoram of Judah | 2 Chronicles 21:12 |
| Anonymous | warned Jehoram of Israel against Arameans | 2 Kings 6:9 |
| Elisha | anointed Hazael king of Damascus | 2 Kings 8:13 |
| | anointed Jehu | 2 Kings 9:1 |
| Elisha | captured an Aramean army | 2 Kings 6:18 |
| | predicted victory | 2 Kings 7:1 |

Before you begin to study these chapters of 1 Kings, review the survey chart on page 19. The following is taken from that chart:

1. J. Barton Payne, *An Outline of Hebrew History* (Grand Rapids: Baker Book House, 1954), pp. 127-28.

| 1:1 | 2:12 | 4:1 | 11:1 | 12:1 | 16:29 | 22 |
|---|---|---|---|---|---|---|
| SOLOMON CROWNED | EARLY DAYS of SOLOMON'S REIGN | Solomon in His Glory | APOSTASY & DEATH | ANTAGONISMS Between ISRAEL & JUDAH | King Ahab and Prophet Elijah | |
| DAVID SUCCEEDED by SOLOMON | | | | ISRAEL CONTEMPORANEOUS with JUDAH | | |
| 40 YEARS | | | | 90 YEARS | | |

## I. ANALYSIS

First read these chapters in one sitting, making notations in your Bible of important words, phrases, characters, actions, and references to God. Write down some of your observations and impressions. Also make your own outline of this passage before referring to the outline shown in this lesson. Locate on a map the major places of this passage, including Sidon (Zidonians), Samaria, Jericho, Tishbe (Tishbite), Brook Cherith, Zarephath, Mount Carmel, Beersheba, Horeb, and Syria.

Next study carefully the accompanying survey chart of this passage. Check to see if each item in the different outlines faithfully represents the test. Notice the following things:

1. The section 16:29-34 is an introduction, by way of furnishing setting, to this story of Elijah.

2. Note the box entitled "God Rebukes Prophet Elijah." In what sense could this also be identified as judgment?

_____

_____

3. Record on the chart the miracles of each of the three main sections.

Keep this chart before you as you proceed now with your analysis on each of the smaller parts, using the following study suggestions:

1. *See 16:29-34 (Ahab).* How is Ahab compared with kings before him?

_____

_____

# THE PROPHET ELIJAH    1 KINGS 16:29—19:21

| SETTING | ACTION | | |
|---|---|---|---|
| AHAB | ELIJAH | | |
| | PROPHECY | ENCOUNTER | FLIGHT |
| MIRACLES: | MIRACLES: | MIRACLES: | MIRACLES: |

| 16:29 / 16:34 | 17:1 | 18:1 | 19:1 | 19:21 |
|---|---|---|---|---|

| MESSAGE and CREDENTIALS of the PROPHET | AUTHORITY and POWER of GOD | FEAR and RETIREMENT of the PROPHET |
|---|---|---|
| 17:1  BROOK  CHERITH | 18:3  THE CONFRONTATION | 19:1 |
| 8  ZAREPHATH | 16  THE CHALLENGE | 9 |
| 24 | 25  THE CONTEST | 15 |
| | 40  THE CONSEQUENCES | 19 |
| | 46 | 21 |

| SINS of ISRAEL | JUDGMENT on the NATION (drought) | JUDGMENT on FALSE PROPHETS (death) | GOD REBUKES PROPHET ELIJAH |
|---|---|---|---|

85

What sins of Ahab are explicitly cited here?

_____

In view of Joshua 6:16, what violation is cited in 1 Kings 16:34?

_____

(Read 34*b* thus: "He laid the foundation thereof *at the cost of* Abiram his firstborn, . . .") Refer to a Bible dictionary for a description of Baal worship (see also *Comments* section).

2. *Chapter 17*. What credentials of a true prophet did Elijah have according to this chapter?

_____

_____

In view of what was involved in Baal worship, how pertinent was the judgment of drought? Read James 5:17, and note what part Elijah played in the judgment of drought. Comparing Luke 4:26 and 1 Kings 17:9, what do you learn about divine sovereignty?

_____

_____

Observe the ways the widow woman, a Gentile, addressed Elijah. Comment on her obedience to Elijah's directions.

_____

Record some of the major points of this chapter on the accompanying chart.

3. *Chapter 18*. Notice the outline of this chapter as shown on the accompanying chart. Record key words and phrases in each paragraph box.

How severe had the drought become? (v. 5)

_____

How did Ahab interpret the drought? (v. 17)

_____

What did Elijah mean by his words, "How long go ye limping between the two sides?"(v. 21, *American Standard Version*)?

_____

What are some of the contrasts of the narrative that follows?

_____

_____

Why did Elijah set up *twelve* stones, in view of the fact that the kingdom was divided?

_____

What are your impressions of Elijah's prayer (vv. 36-37)?

_____

Why were the prophets of Baal slain? (cf. Deut. 13:13-15; 1 Kings 18:4, 13)

_____

_____

4. *Chapter 19.* As you study this chapter paragraph by paragraph, record observations on the accompanying chart. (You may choose to make a more extended study of this chapter by recording on a larger analytical chart.) What important practical lessons may be learned from this experience of Elijah?

_____

_____

Comment on each of the phrases cited below. Do not overlook any hidden meanings or implications in the phrases.
- (a) "O Lord, take away my life" (v. 4)
- (b) "Then an angel touched him" (v. 5)
- (c) "What doest thou here, Elijah" (vv. 9, 13)
- (d) "I, even I only, am left" (vv. 10, 14)
- (e) "The Lord was not in the earthquake" (v. 11)

(f) "A still small voice" (v. 12)

(g) "I have left me seven thousand in Israel" (v. 18)

Concerning the reference of 19:17 "shall Elisha slay": this meant slaying by the word of the Lord. Compare similar references in Isaiah 11:4; 49:2; and Revelation 1:16.

5. Before reading the comments that follow, write out a list of the main spiritual lessons you have learned from this passage.

_____

_____

_____

_____

_____

## II. COMMENTS

Ahab, the seventh to occupy the throne of Israel, was worse than all those who had gone before him. Not only did he "walk in the sins of Jeroboam," sanctioning the calf worship and other iniquities that prevailed, but with his marriage to Jezebel, the daughter of the priest of Baal, he introduced Israel to Baal worship with all its loathsome and licentious rites. And he himself also became a Baal worshiper. This was his greatest sin.

Baal ("master") was the name given by various nations to their presiding gods. The Baal of Tyre was Melkarth, their chief god. "Melkarth was the king of gods that required the burning of innocent children as oblations upon his altar. One of the underlying reasons that Baal was worshiped was that he was believed to be lord of the land. To induce him to send rain upon the earth, fertility cult practices were engaged in and sacrifices were offered."[2] On the sacrifice of children, read Jeremiah 19:5.

Upon this scene of complete departure from God, Elijah suddenly appeared before Ahab out of the wild and rugged hills of Gilead. Without apology or preamble he hurled a message from Jehovah at the wicked king. If Ahab had been familiar with the writings of Moses he would have known that this was just what God had determined would be the punishment upon His people for worshiping false deities. (See Deut. 11:16-17.)

The history of Elijah should be carefully pondered. It affords much encouragement and instruction for servants of God in all

2. Charles F. Pfeiffer and Everett F. Harrison, eds., _The Wycliffe Bible Commentary_ (Chicago: Moody, 1962), p. 330.

ages. Today we live in times not wholly dissimilar to those in which Elijah lived. Now, as then, false religions flourish; sin and apostasy are rampant; the majority of people are living with little or no recognition of God. And as followers of God we are called upon, as was Elijah, to live close to Him, giving a clear witness to the truth whenever opportunity affords, and patiently learning the lessons God would teach us.

Four chapters in 1 Kings (chaps. 17-19 and 21) tell principally of Elijah. In chapter 17 we see Elijah, after his sudden appearance and brief message to Ahab, retiring to private life and being trained by God for his great work. In chapter 18 we see him in public as he stands on Mount Carmel and by his mighty faith and prayer turns an erring nation back to God. In chapter 19 we see him again in private, being ministered to in his despair and being instructed and recommissioned; and in chapter 21 we see him delivering God's final messages to Israel's wicked king Ahab.

### A. Elijah Before Ahab

Picture this rough-clad messenger of Jehovah addressing the richly attired, luxury-loving king. Notice carefully Elijah's words "As the Lord God of Israel liveth." Ignored and forgotten as He was throughout the land, the Lord God of Israel was *living* and was about to make His power felt. To this living God Elijah had been earnestly praying that He would fulfill the warning of Deuteronomy 11:16-17, probably in the hope that this chastisement of a drought might be sufficient to turn all Israel from Baal worship back to God. A. C. Gaebelein says, "It was in secret that he sought God's presence and wrestled in prayer, until the Lord sent him forth with the message of judgment. Prayer, persevering prayer, is the one great need in these days of declension and departure from God, and is the one resource of God's faithful ones."

Notice also Elijah's words "Before whom I stand." This phrase is used to describe service. Elijah was in the service of the living God. F. B. Meyer says, "He was standing in the presence of Ahab; but he was conscious of the presence of One greater than any earthly monarch, even the presence of Jehovah. . . . Let us cultivate this habitual recognition of the presence of God; it will lift us above all earthly fear."

The name Elijah means "Jehovah is my God," and though all Israel might bow the knee to Baal, Elijah by his name and by his life proclaimed his unfaltering allegiance to Lord God of Israel.

## B. At the Brook Cherith, and Zarephath

Next we see Elijah obeying God's command by hiding himself by the Brook Cherith somewhere on the east side of the Jordan River. What lessons Elijah must have learned in that solitary place—lessons of faith and patience and of God's power to provide. As morning by morning and evening by evening the ravens brought him bread and flesh, and as he drank of the brook and watched it growing drier and drier, he must have learned to trust God absolutely. He learned about the omnipotence of the God who could give a command and compel ravens to do that which was contrary to their nature. A miracle, yes, but as F. B. Meyer says, "the presence of the supernatural presents no difficulties to those who can say 'Our Father.'"

After leaving this retreat by the Brook Cherith, Elijah went to Zarephath, a port city between Tyre and Sidon, where he was sustained with his hostess and her son for many days by miraculously supplied meal and oil. The miracle of restoring the life of the dead boy took place there.

These wonderful experiences at Zarephath must have greatly strengthened Elijah's faith in the power of God. He needed to have absolute and unwavering faith for the great encounter that was coming. These experiences also must have turned the heart of both the widow and her son to the Lord God of Israel. Note the widow's words after her son had been brought back from the dead (1 Kings 17:24).

## C. The Contest

Ahab and Elijah were brought together again, this time by Obadiah, steward of Ahab's castle. Obadiah (not the author of the Bible book) "feared the Lord greatly" and had proved his sincerity and piety by what he did, but he also stood in fear of Ahab's displeasure. Obadiah had nothing of Elijah's impregnable faith, nothing of his holy boldness or wide vision.

The meeting between Elijah and Ahab was dramatic. Obadiah and the persecuted sons of the prophets might cringe with fear before the infuriated monarch, but not Elijah. Strong in the consciousness of the living God, Elijah boldly answered the faithless king, "I have not troubled Israel; but thou, and thy father's house, in that ye have forsaken the commandments of the Lord, and thou hast followed Baalim" (1 Kings 18:18). H. J. Carpenter says that then Elijah challenged the king to 'put an end to the sinful indecision by which he had brought ruin to the nation, and to let the great question be definitely settled whether or not Jehovah was to be the recognized God of Israel."

Elijah probably chose Mount Carmel as the place for the "battle of the gods" because it was "debatable ground between Israel and Phoenicia, and was held sacred to the Canaanite gods."[3] "If this interpretation be correct, Elijah, like saints before and after him, dared to do battle with 'the spirit of wickedness in high places.'"[4]

Elijah manifested implicit confidence that God would prove Himself to be indeed the living God. With prophetic authority he derided the priests of Baal, purposely using twelve stones to build the altar to remind the Israelites that a unified, not a divided, nation was the will of God.

When the mighty victory came and Elijah saw the multitude on their faces, acknowledging the truth and crying, "The Lord, he is the God; the Lord, he is the God," he did not rest until the false prophets were put to death, and the rain descended in torrents. The judgment of death for the false prophets partly avenged Jezebel's slaying of the true prophets and partly was the penalty for violation of God's law (Deut. 13:13-15).

## D. Elijah Flees

The next picture we have of Elijah is that of a man physically exhausted, thoroughly frightened, terribly discouraged, and running for his life from Jezreel to the wilderness. God's tender care of His overwrought prophet is clearly evident. No rebuke for his lapse of faith in God or for his fear of Jezebel, or for leaving his post of duty just when he was so needed as a leader in Israel. Just sleep and food and an angel ministering to him. "Like as a father pitieth his children, so the Lord pitieth them that fear him" (Ps. 103:13).

But God had further work to do in Elijah's heart. Elijah had gone to Horeb, a mountain in the vicinity of Mount Sinai. While he was in a cave there God spoke to him, giving him reproof, challenge, encouragement, and a new commission. Prominent in the narrative is the fact that it was not the strong wind or the earthquake or the fire, but the still small voice that caused Elijah to cover his face. He recognized the nearness of God and could not stand uncovered in His presence.

God's program with Israel was not over, and God wanted Elijah to know that His purposes would continue to be fulfilled

3. Francis Davidson, ed., *The New Bible Commentary* (Grand Rapids: Eerdmans, 1953), p. 315.
4. Pfeiffer and Harrison, ibid., p. 332.

through human instruments—some good and some bad—as before. Elijah had more work to do; the sword of a foreign king (Hazael) would cut down many; the throne of a king of Israel (Jehu) would bring civil strife; the word of a prophet (Elisha) would spell the decrees of a sovereign God; and a remnant (seven thousand) would keep alive a fellowship between God and faithful souls.

## III. SUMMARY

As an exercise, review your study of these chapters, and write a brief summary of their contents.

# Lesson 10

# Alliance

The book of 1 Kings has no structural conclusion from a literary standpoint, since in the original writing 1 Kings and 2 Kings were one book. Thus the passage found in chapters 20-22 is neither climax, summary, nor conclusion to the preceding chapters. The next study manual in this series continues the study of Kings from this point in the narrative, as though no major break exists. The accompanying brief outline shows one way in which 2 Kings emerges out of 1 Kings during the era labeled ALLIANCES. (See Lesson 8.)

## HE COEXISTING KINGDOMS of ISRAEL and JUDAH

| ANTAGONISMS | ALLIANCES | ANTAGONISMS |
|---|---|---|
| 1 Kings 12 | 1 Kings 16:29 | 2 Kings 13:10 |
| | | 2 Kings 17 |

The ministry of the prophet Elijah to the prophets of Baal and King Ahab was the subject of our study in Lesson 9. In this lesson we shall study more about evil Ahab of Israel; about good King Jehoshaphat who reigned over Judah contemporaneously with Ahab; and about an alliance between the two.

As we study the history of the kings of Israel and Judah and observe God's frequent interpositions, we must constantly bear in mind His *purposes* in dealing with His people. Remember that God had selected Israel to be a witness to Himself among the nations of the world, and He would not lightly abandon that pur-

| AHAB (1 Kings 20:1—21:29, 22:37-40) | |
|---|---|
| MAIN FACTS | TRUTHS TAUGHT |
| | |

| JEHOSHAPHAT (1 Kings 22:41-50; 2 Chron. 17:1-19; 19:1—21:1 | |
|---|---|
| MAIN FACTS | TRUTHS TAUGHT |
| | |

| THE ALLIANCE (1 Kings 22:1-36; 2 Chron. 18:1-34) | |
|---|---|
| MAIN FACTS | TRUTHS TAUGHT |
| | |

pose. Therefore, all His chastisements for sin, all His manifestations of power and mercy, and all His messages were to this end. They were efforts to turn the people back to Himself and fit them for the high calling for which He had designed the nation. If we overlook this fact we miss one of the major purposes of these historical books in telling the story of God's long and patient forbearance with this rebellious people.

## I. ANALYSIS

For the analysis of this final lesson, use methods and approaches of your own choosing. Keep in mind these three processes of Bible study: observation, interpretation, application.

Study this lesson in three units: Ahab, Jehoshaphat, and the alliance between the two. One simple approach is to record main facts and main truths taught, which may be recorded on the accompanying chart.

Another approach to this lesson is to study the sins and judgments of this narrative. Follow this broad outline:

1. First sin of Ahab; and judgment (chap. 20)
2. Second sin of Ahab; and judgment (chap. 21)
3. The sins of prophets and of the alliance; and judgment (22:1-40)

## II. COMMENTS

### A. Ahab

Some time after the great decision day on Mount Carmel, the king of Syria, Ben-hadad, gathered all his armies and went up and besieged Samaria. One would naturally suppose that Ahab, who had just seen God's power exhibited and His willingness to answer prayer, would have immediately called for God's aid against these opposing armies. Instead, he called upon the elders for their advice.

But God sought to convince Ahab that He is indeed the Lord. Though unasked, God promised His help in the coming battle. As always, God faithfully fulfilled His promise and gave Ahab the victory. Then, as if to further assure Ahab of His willingness to give aid, God sent a message by a prophet (1 Kings 20:22). In the next Syrian campaign against Israel, about a year after the first, God gave Israel the victory again, that both the Syrians and Ahab might know "that I am the Lord" (1 Kings 20:28).

A. C. Gaebelein says, "But after all this Ahab let Ben-hadad, who had defied Jehovah, live. More than that he treated him like a friend and brother, had him come into his chariot and made a covenant with him. In showing such clemency to the enemy of God, Ahab revealed the state of his soul. He had no heart for the Lord, and was bound to follow his own wicked ways." (Read 1 Kings 20:35-43.) Notice the stern rebuke and judgment from God that was brought to Ahab by the prophet.

In chapter 21 we see Ahab again exhibiting utter disregard for God's will and entirely bent on having his own way. He cared nothing for the law that God had made governing the transfer of land from one tribe to another. (Cf. 1 Kings 21:1-3 with Lev. 25:23-28 and Num. 36:7-8.) Naboth, on the other hand, respected God's law. Although Ahab did not actually participate in his murder, nevertheless he was glad for it and offered no word of rebuke to his diabolical queen, who had perpetrated this crime (1 Kings 21:5-16). Notice that in God's sight Ahab himself was considered the murderer (1 Kings 21:18-19).

Ahab's last encounter with Elijah did not fill the self-willed king with repentance but with rage (1 Kings 21:17-20). Elijah's pronouncement of God's judgment on Ahab was severe. Every male descendant of Ahab was to die, and his house was to suffer the same fate as those of Jeroboam and Baasha (1 Kings 21:17-20). Two dynasties in Israel had been destroyed because of their presumptuous and persistent sin against God; now the third dynasty was to suffer a like fate and the fourth dynasty put on trial. But note how merciful God is. Because Ahab humbled himself, God lightened the sentence by postponing the predicted doom until after his death (1 Kings 21:27-29).

From Ahab's actions in 1 Kings 21:27 one might think that at last he was repentant and would turn wholly to God. But in the closing chapter of the book, where we get our final glimpse of this king of Israel, there is no suggestion of submission to God or repentance for sin.

After three years of peace between Syria and Israel, Ahab determined to take Ramoth in Gilead by force from the king of Syria. Ramoth was one of the cities that Ben-hadad had failed to restore to Israel as he had promised. (Cf. 1 Kings 20:34 and 1 Kings 22:1-3.)

At that time the pious and noble-hearted Jehoshaphat was reigning over Judah. His son had married the daughter of Ahab and Jezebel, and Jehoshaphat had come to Samaria to visit the king of Israel. Ahab took this occasion to invite him to join in the battle against Syria. Jehoshaphat consented but requested Ahab to seek the counsel of the Lord (1 Kings 22:4-5).

The four hundred prophets whom Ahab gathered together were not reliable prophets. Even though they were false prophets, they used Jehovah's name just as constantly as the men who had not forsaken His commandments. No doubt they were eager for court favor and told the king what they knew he wanted to hear (1 Kings 22:6).

King Jehoshaphat sensed that these men were not true prophets of Jehovah. Note his question and Ahab's answer in 1 Kings 22:7-8. Even Ahab recognized the difference between Micaiah and the rest of the prophets gathered there. Micaiah was in prison because he had faithfully preached the word of God.

Note the temptation put before Micaiah and how he met it (1 Kings 22:9-14). Micaiah's words in verse 15 were spoken in sarcasm, mimicking the words of the four hundred false prophets; but when the king demanded the truth, he told him the revelation that he had received (1 Kings 22:15-28).

In the battle that followed we see the life of Jehoshaphat miraculously (not accidentally) spared, and Ahab miraculously (not accidentally) slain by a man who drew his bow "at a venture" (i.e., without any particular target in mind). The arrow was guided by a higher hand. It found the small opening in the harness of the disguised king of Israel.

Ahab, when wounded, was taken from the fighting line. He bravely stayed in his chariot and directed his army until evening, when he died (1 Kings 22:29-40; cf. 2 Chron. 18:1-34).

### B. Jehoshaphat

In 1 Kings only ten verses are written of Jehoshaphat's reign, but in 2 Chronicles a much fuller account is given of the life of this righteous and influential king. A glance at the chart on page 102 will show that he was reigning in Judah for twenty-five years, during which time three different kings—Ahab, Ahaziah, and Joram —reigned in Israel. When Jehoshaphat became king of Judah at age thirty-five, Ahab had been reigning over Israel for about four years (1 Kings 22:41-42).

Jehoshaphat began his reign by strengthening himself against Israel. However, his source of strength lay in the fact that the Lord was with him; and the Lord was with him because he was true to the Lord. (Read 2 Chron. 17:1-6.)

Jehoshaphat desired his people to walk as he himself was walking in the ways of his father David. He wanted them to have strong faith in God. Knowing the truth that "faith cometh by hearing, and hearing by the word of God," (Rom. 10:17), he instituted a movement for the instruction of his people that could not fail to bring about remarkable and beneficial results. (Read 2 Chron. 17:6-9.)

Note that this was a nationwide revival in Bible study. The instructors were the leading men of the nation—princes, Levites, and priests. They took the book of the law of the Lord with them and taught it in all the cities of Judah. Now notice the material results that followed in addition to the spiritual results, which we shall notice later. There was peace with all the surrounding nations (2 Chron. 17:10); the income of the nation was greatly increased (2 Chron. 17:11); there was a tremendous revival in building and in business generally throughout the cities of Judah (2 Chron. 17:12-13); and in Jerusalem there was a large standing army (2 Chron. 17:13-19). James M. Gray says, "These verses show that no monarch since Solomon equaled Jehoshaphat in the extent of his revenue, the strength of his fortifications and the number of his troops. It pays to serve God."

There was usually war between the kingdom of Judah and Israel, but we read that Jehoshaphat made peace with the king of Israel (1 Kings 22:44; 2 Chron. 18:1).

Peace between these kingdoms was desirable, but it was all too temporary. For, as we shall see, one thing led to another until eventually Jehoshaphat found himself in entanglements, from the effects of which his kingdom never fully recovered. Being at peace with the king of Israel, Jehoshaphat went to visit him and became involved in a battle with the Syrians in which he nearly lost his life. This we studied in the last lesson, and it is also recorded in chapter 18 of 2 Chronicles. Later, as we shall see, he engaged in a business venture in partnership with the king of Israel, and his ships were wrecked.

But worse than all else, Jehoshaphat's son married the daughter of Ahab and Jezebel (2 Chron. 21:6). This young princess, Athaliah, was much like her mother, Jezebel. When she became queen in Judah she introduced Baal worship and almost succeeded in destroying all the royal seed of the line of David. Joining affinity with the wicked always brings disastrous results. God's will for His children has always been separation—"Be ye not unequally yoked together with unbelievers" (2 Cor. 6:14).

Apparently Jehoshaphat had not willfully intended to displease the Lord when he made an alliance with Ahab. Nevertheless, on his return to Jerusalem from his visit to the king of Israel, a sharp rebuke from God awaited him (2 Chron. 19:1-3). Jehoshaphat made no reply, but his actions indicate that true repentance took place in his heart (2 Chron. 19:4-11).

Jehoshaphat then proceeded to appoint judges throughout the land of Judah. What a blessing it would be in any community today to have judges who followed King Jehoshaphat's instructions. Notice that they were commanded to judge "not for man, but for the Lord" (2 Chron. 19:6); there was to be justice that was not blinded by respect of persons or the taking of bribes (2 Chron. 19:7); and they were to judge faithfully and with a perfect heart (2 Chron. 19:9).

After years of peace Judah was threatened by the Moabites and the Ammonites, who invaded the land with a great host (2 Chron. 20:1-2). Note how Jehoshaphat and the men of Judah met this crisis. Instead of mustering his fighting men for defense or calling on any other nation for help, Jehoshaphat went straight to God in prayer, and his people followed him (2 Chron. 20:3-4). Jehoshaphat himself led this great prayer meeting—and what a prayer he made.

Study Jehoshaphat's prayer (2 Chron. 20:5-12), and observe its elements of strength. Note how he addressed the Lord, acknowledging His sovereignty and omnipotence (vv. 5-6). Note how he recalled God's past dealings with His people (vv. 7-9. Note how he laid the great need of the people and their own helplessness before God (vv. 10-12). Note that "all Judah stood before the Lord" (v. 13)—the men, the women and the children all attended this prayer meeting.

This is the sort of praying that prevails, and God immediately sent His answer through Jahaziel (2 Chron. 20:14-17). Note also that Jehoshaphat and his people did not fail to have a praise and thanksgiving meeting also (2 Chron. 20:18-19).

Humanly speaking the whole preparation for this battle would appear most strange. Jehoshaphat's only charge to the army was for them to have faith in God and in His word (2 Chron. 20:20). In front of the soldiers marched singers pouring out praises to God (2 Chron. 20:21). God had told His people that they would not have to fight in this battle in order to win it. He marvelously fulfilled His promise (2 Chron. 20:17, 22-25). Without striking a blow or losing a man, Jehoshaphat and his people found their enemies vanquished and slain, and themselves in possession of such vast spoil that it took them three days to remove it. It pays to trust and obey God.

Before beginning their triumphal return to Jerusalem, Jehoshaphat and his people gathered in the valley of Berachah for a thanksgiving service, and on their arrival at Jerusalem they went straight to the Temple, probably for more prayer and praise (2 Chron. 20:26-28). See the far-reaching effect of this manifestation of faith on the part of God's people (2 Chron. 20:29-30).

If Jehoshaphat's history could have ended with what we are told in 2 Chronicles 20:31-34, there would have been little in his reign to criticize. But two more incidents in his life are recorded —two alliances that he made with the wicked sons of Ahab. One alliance was for the purpose of commerce and one for the purpose of war, and both were displeasing to the Lord.

Years before, Jehoshaphat had joined with Ahab against the Syrians in an attempt to regain Ramoth in Gilead. God had sharply rebuked him for this through the prophet Jehu (2 Chron. 19:1-2). Ahab had died, and his wicked son Ahaziah was on the throne of Israel (1 Kings 22:51-53). It is sad to see a man like Jehoshaphat joining in a business venture with a man like King Ahaziah, but read what is said in 2 Chronicles 20:35-36. This brought forth another rebuke from the Lord and also disaster to his business venture (2 Chron. 20:37). It seems from 1 Kings 22:49 that there was another attempt to engage Jehoshaphat in a business expedition, in which he refused to become involved. The account of Jehoshaphat's alliance with another son of Ahab for the purpose of war is described in chapter 3 of 2 Kings, which is covered in the next study manual.

So Jehoshaphat's reign did not come to an end without some blemishes. But, like his father, Asa, he was accepted of God because when he sinned, he acknowledged his sin. Only for such a heart could it be said of him that he did "that which was right in the sight of the Lord."

The last four verses of 1 Kings record briefly the evil reign of Ahaziah, Israel's sixth king. The next book of 2 Kings opens with a story about this king and the prophet Elijah.

| KINGS OF ISRAEL | YEARS* OF REIGN | CHARACTER | RELATIONS WITH JUDAH | DETHRONED BY | HISTORY |
|---|---|---|---|---|---|
| 1 JEROBOAM | 22 | Bad | War | | 1 Kings 11:26—14:20<br>2 Chronicles 9:29—13:22 |
| 2 NADAB | 2 | Bad | War | Baasha | 1 Kings 15:25-28 |
| 3 BAASHA | 24 | Bad | War | | 1 Kings 15:27—16:7<br>2 Chronicles 6:1-6 |
| 4 ELAH | 2 | Drunkard | War | Zimri | 2 Kings 16:8-10 |
| 5 ZIMRI | 7 days | Murderer | War | Omri | 1 Kings 16:10-20 |
| 6 OMRI | 12 | Very Bad | War | | 1 Kings 16:16-27 |
| 7 AHAB | 22 | Exceedingly Wicked | Alliance | | 1 Kings 16:28—22:40<br>2 Chronicles 18:1-34 |
| 8 AHAZIAH | 2 | Bad | Peace | | 1 Kings 22:40, 51-53<br>2 Kings 1:1-17<br>2 Chronicles 20:35-37 |
| 9 JORAM | 12 | Bad | Alliance | Jehu | 2 Kings 3:1-3; 9:14-25<br>2 Chronicles 22:5-7 |
| 10 JEHU | 28 | Bad | War | | 2 Kings 9:1—10:36<br>2 Chronicles 22:7-12 |
| 11 JEHOAHAZ | 17 | Bad | Peace | | 2 Kings 13:1-9 |
| 12 JEHOASH | 16 | Bad | War | | 2 King 13:10-25; 14:8-16<br>2 Chronicles 25:17-24 |
| 13 JEROBOAM II | 41 | Bad | Peace | | 2 Kings 14:23-29 |
| 14 ZECHARIAH | 6 months | Bad | Peace | Shallum | 2 Kings 15:8-12 |
| 15 SHALLUM | 1 month | Bad | Peace | Menahem | 2 Kings 15:13-15 |
| 16 MENAHEM | 10 | Bad | Peace | | 2 Kings 15:16-22 |
| 17 PEKAHIAH | 2 | Bad | Peace | Pekah | 2 Kings 15:23-26 |
| 18 PEKAH | 20 | Bad | War | Hoshea | 2 Kings 15:27-31<br>2 Chronicles 28:5-8 |
| 19 HOSHEA | 9 | Bad | Peace | | 2 Kings 17:1-41 |

* These figures, as recorded in the biblical text, do not always reflect coregencies of kings. (Same applies to the table on p. 109.) The "Chart of Kings and Prophets" (pp. 110-11) shows all the coregencies.

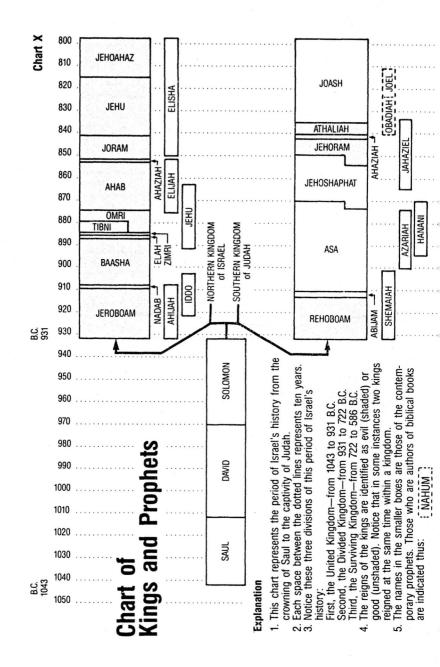

# Chart of Kings and Prophets

**Chart X**

## Explanation

1. This chart represents the period of Israel's history from the crowning of Saul to the captivity of Judah.
2. Each space between the dotted lines represents ten years.
3. Notice these three divisions of this period of Israel's history:
   First, the United Kingdom—from 1043 to 931 B.C.
   Second, the Divided Kingdom—from 931 to 722 B.C.
   Third, the Surviving Kingdom—from 722 to 586 B.C.
4. The reigns of the kings are identified as evil (shaded) or good (unshaded). Notice that in some instances two kings reigned at the same time within a kingdom.
5. The names in the smaller boxes are those of the contemporary prophets. Those who are authors of biblical books are indicated thus: NAHUM

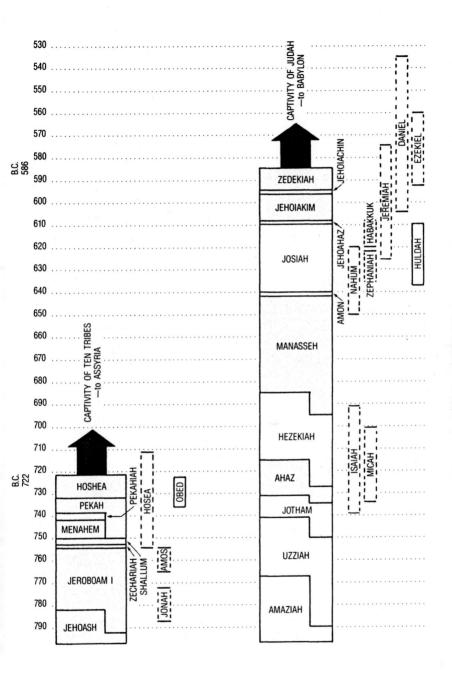

B.C.
586

B.C.
722

530
540
550
560
570
580
590
600
610
620
630
640
650
660
670
680
690
700
710
720
730
740
750
760
770
780
790

CAPTIVITY OF JUDAH
—to BABYLON

CAPTIVITY OF TEN TRIBES
—to ASSYRIA

ZEDEKIAH
JEHOIAKIM
JOSIAH
MANASSEH
HEZEKIAH
AHAZ
JOTHAM
UZZIAH
AMAZIAH

JEHOIACHIN
JEHOAHAZ
AMON

HOSHEA
PEKAH
MENAHEM
JEROBOAM I
JEHOASH

PEKAHIAH
ZECHARIAH
SHALLUM

HOSEA
OBED
AMOS
JONAH

DANIEL
EZEKIEL
JEREMIAH
HABAKKUK
ZEPHANIAH
NAHUM
HULDAH
ISAIAH
MICAH

103

# KINGS OF JUDAH

| KINGS OF JUDAH | AGE BEGAN REIGNING | YEARS OF REIGN | CHARACTER | RELATIONS WITH ISRAEL | HISTORY |
|---|---|---|---|---|---|
| 1 REHOBOAM | 41 | 17 | Bad | War | 1 Kings 12:1—14:31<br>2 Chronicles 10:1—12:16 |
| 2 ABIJAM | | 3 | Bad | War | 1 Kings 15:1-8<br>2 Chronicles 13:1-22 |
| 3 ASA | | 41 | Good | War | 1 Kings 15:9-24<br>2 Chronicles 14:1—16:14 |
| 4 JEHOSHAPHAT | 35 | 25 | Good | Peace | 1 Kings 22:41-50<br>2 Chronicles 17:1—20:37 |
| 5 JEHORAM | 32 | 8 | Bad | Peace | 2 Kings 8:16-24<br>2 Chronicles 21:1-20 |
| 6 AHAZIAH | 22 | 1 | Bad | Alliance | 2 Kings 8:25-29; 9:27-29<br>2 Chronicles 22:1-9 |
| 7 ATHALIAH (queen) | | 6 | Bad | Peace | 2 Kings 8:18, 25-28; 11:1-20<br>2 Chronicles 22:1—23:21; 24:7 |
| 8 JOASH | 7 | 40 | Good | Peace | 2 Kings 11:1—12:21<br>2 Chronicles 22:10—24:27 |
| 9 AMAZIAH | 25 | 29 | Good | War | 2 Kings 14:1-14<br>2 Chronicles 25:1-28 |
| 10 UZZIAH (Azariah) | 16 | 52 | Good | Peace | 2 Kings 15:1-7<br>2 Chronicles 26:1-23 |
| 11 JOTHAM | 25 | 16 | Good | War | 2 Kings 15:32-28<br>2 Chronicles 27:1-9 |
| 12 AHAZ | 20 | 16 | Bad | War | 2 Kings 16:1-20<br>2 Chronicles 28:1-27 |
| 13 HEZEKIAH | 25 | 29 | Good | | 2 Kings 18:1—20:21<br>2 Chronicles 29:1—32:33 |
| 14 MANASSEH | 12 | 55 | Bad | | 2 Kings 21:1-18<br>2 Chronicles 33:1-20 |
| 15 AMON | 22 | 2 | Bad | | 2 Kings 21:19-23<br>2 Chronicles 33:21-25 |
| 16 JOSIAH | 8 | 31 | Good | | 2 Kings 22:1—23:30<br>2 Chronicles 34:1—35:27 |
| 17 JEHOAHAZ | 23 | 3 months | Bad | | 2 Kings 23:31-33<br>2 Chronicles 36:1-4 |
| 18 JEHOIAKIM | 25 | 11 | Bad | | 2 Kings 23:34—24:5<br>2 Chronicles 36:5-7 |
| 19 JEHOIACHIN | 18 | 3 months | Bad | | 2 Kings 24:6-16<br>2 Chronicles 36:8-10 |
| 20 ZEDEKIAH | 21 | 11 | Bad | | 2 Kings 24:17—25:7<br>2 Chronicles 36:11-21 |

# Summary of 1 Kings

In our study of 1 Kings (and the parallel passages of Chronicles) we have watched a prosperous and strong nation choosing to go its own way and reaping the judgments of disruption, war, and sorrows.

Half of 1 Kings is devoted to the reign of the last of the three kings of the united kingdom, Solomon: his coronation, administration, building of the Temple, apostasy, and death. Solomon cherished the privilege of building such a beautiful temple for the "dwelling place" of God, and in the course of this project it could be said that Solomon was truly in his glory. But he was not careful about the temple of his *heart*, and in his last three years he "did evil in the sight of the Lord, and went not fully after the Lord, as did David his father." The consequences of judgment were drastic: The kingdom was split, with ten tribes (Israel) in the north banded together under evil kings ruling out of Samaria, and two tribes (Judah) remaining true to the Davidic line, ruled by kings on the throne at Jerusalem, some of whom were good, and some evil.

The narrative of the last half of 1 Kings alternates back and forth between the two kingdoms, recording the sins and the troubles of these peoples. Two elements of the story are the good reigns of two of Judah's kings, Asa and Jehoshaphat, and of the prophet of God Elijah. There is no main concluding section to the book of 1 Kings, for the simple reason that in the original writing 1 Kings and 2 Kings were one book. The study of 2 Kings therefore picks up the narrative where 1 Kings leaves off.

The first book of Kings teaches that government by man, with God left out, leads to disaster; and also that the grace of God, with man in mind, preserves a remnant. That remnant of believers is God's unbroken witness to all generations that the Lord is the true King.

# Bibliography

## RESOURCES FOR FURTHER STUDY

Crockett, William Day. *A Harmony of the Books of Samuel, Kings and Chronicles.* Grand Rapids: Baker, 1954.

Douglas, J. D., ed. *The New Bible Dictionary.* Grand Rapids: Eerdmans, 1962.

Eason, J. Lawrence. *The New Bible Survey.* Grand Rapids: Zondervan, 1963.

Jensen, Irving L. *Jensen's Survey of the Old Testament.* Chicago: Moody, 1978.

*New International Version Study Bible.* Grand Rapids: Zondervan, 1985.

*Ryrie Study Bible.* Chicago: Moody, 1985

Strong, James. *The Exhaustive Concordance of the Bible.* New York: Abingdon, 1890.

Unger, Merrill F. *New Unger's Bible Dictionary.* Chicago: Moody, 1988.

Young, Edward J. *An Introduction to the Old Testament.* Grand Rapids: Eerdmans, 1949.


## COMMENTARIES AND TOPICAL STUDIES

Douglas, J. D., ed. *New Bible Dictionary.* Grand Rapids: Eerdmans, 1962.

Ellison, H. L. "1 and 2 Kings" and "1 and 2 Chronicles." In *The New Bible Commentary,* ed. F. Davidson. Grand Rapids: Eerdmans, 1953.

Gates, John T., and Stigers, Harold. "First and Second Kings." In *The Wycliffe Bible Commentary,* ed. Charles F. Pfeiffer and Everett F. Harrison. Chicago: Moody, 1962.

Kirk, Thomas, and George Rawlinson. *Studies in the Book of Kings.* 2 vols. Minneapolis: Klock and Klock, 1983.

Payne, J. Barton. "1 and 2 Chronicles." In *The Wycliffe Bible Commentary,* ed. Charles F. Pfeiffer and Everett F. Harrison. Chicago: Moody, 1962.

Samuel. *The Old Testament Speaks.* New York: Harper, 1940.

John C. *Solomon to the Exile: Studies in Kings and Chronicles.* Grand Rapids: Baker, 1971.